Be a Builder in the Kingdom

The C.E.M.E.N.T. Guide to Creating a Lasting Legacy

Gerard Assey

Be a Builder in the Kingdom:
The C.E.M.E.N.T. Guide
to Creating a Lasting Legacy
By
Gerard Assey

Published by:
Gerard Assey
19/18, Palli Arasan Street
Anna Nagar East
Chennai - 600 102

ISBN: 978-81-974369-3-2

(Image courtesy Starline on Freepik at: www.Freepik.com-Thank You)

Table of Contents

Acknowledgement and Honor

This book was inspired by a powerful message shared by my Spiritual Father, Prophet Jerome Fernando, on Celebration Sunday, May 26th, 2024. His sermon ignited a profound desire within me to create a guide that fosters a builder's mindset and mentality in others.

For nearly a decade, I have had the privilege of listening to and following this remarkable Man of God, who has been more than a Spiritual Father to me. He has also served as my Mentor and Life Coach, consistently delivering revelations that elevate and transform lives. His wisdom, guidance, and unwavering dedication have been a source of inspiration and a model for countless souls, including myself.

Thank you, Father, for your relentless commitment to God's work and for being a beacon of light and hope. Your influence has shaped this work, and I am deeply grateful for all you have done and continue to do in our lives.

Preface

In a world where many are content with merely existing, a select few choose the path of building—creating, sustaining, and leaving a legacy that endures for generations. This book, **"Be a Builder in the Kingdom: *The C.E.M.E.N.T. Guide to Creating a Lasting Legacy,"*** is a call to all who aspire to be more than mere spectators in life. It is an invitation to embrace the divine calling of being builders in God's Kingdom, a calling rooted deeply in biblical principles and exemplified through the lives of faithful men and women in Scripture.

The inspiration for this book was ignited during a Celebration Sunday message shared by my Spiritual Father, Prophet Jerome Fernando, on May 26, 2024. His profound insights on having a builder's mindset resonated with me deeply, compelling me to delve further into what it truly means to build with Purpose, Passion, and Perseverance.

"Being a Kingdom Builder" is structured around the six essential ingredients encapsulated in the acronym C.E.M.E.N.T.: **C**ontinuity, **E**stablishment, **M**emorial, **E**ndure, **N**oble Purpose, and **T**imelessness. Each ingredient represents a foundational aspect of building something of eternal value, something that not only stands the test of time but also honors God and serves His Kingdom.

As you journey through the chapters of this book, you will explore how God Himself is the ultimate builder, as declared in Hebrews 3:3-4: *"For every house is built by someone, but God is the builder of everything."* You will learn how being created in His image (Genesis 1:27) calls us to mirror His attributes as builders in our personal lives, families, communities, and beyond.

This book is not just a theoretical exploration but a practical guide filled with actionable steps, real-life examples, and biblical wisdom. From the rebuilding efforts of Nehemiah to Jesus' establishment of the church, we will uncover the timeless truths and strategies that can transform us into effective builders.

Furthermore, we will address the common hindrances and opposing forces that deter many from building, providing strategies to overcome these challenges. We will categorize people into Survival Oriented, Maintenance Oriented, and Growth Oriented, and explore the significance of being Problem Solvers and History Makers rather than Problem Watchers and History Readers.

"Be a Builder in the Kingdom: *The C.E.M.E.N.T. Guide to Creating a Lasting Legacy,"* is a journey of transformation. It is about developing a mindset that sees beyond the immediate and the mundane, envisioning a future that reflects God's glory and His purposes. It is about understanding that building is not just an activity but a way of life, an honorable pursuit that leaves a lasting impact.

My prayer is that as you read this book, you will be inspired, equipped, and empowered to take up the mantle of a builder. May you find the courage to start, the wisdom to continue, and the faith to finish.

Let us build together, not just for ourselves, but for the generations to come and for the eternal Kingdom of God.

Blessings,

Understanding the Concept of Building

The act of building is fundamental to the human experience and profoundly rooted in the Bible. Building involves creating something of lasting value, whether it is a physical structure, a relationship, a community, or a legacy. In the biblical context, building is not merely a physical act but a spiritual and divine one, reflecting God's character and purpose. When we build, we participate in God's ongoing creation, manifesting His glory and purposes in our lives and the world around us.

In the Scriptures, building is often associated with obedience, faith, and divine guidance. For instance, Noah built the ark under God's instruction, demonstrating his faith and obedience (Genesis 6:14-22). Likewise, Moses followed God's detailed plans to build the tabernacle, a dwelling place for God among His people (Exodus 25-31). These biblical narratives illustrate that building according to God's design brings His presence and blessings.

Moreover, building in the Kingdom of God transcends physical structures. It encompasses building lives, communities, and legacies that honor God. As believers, we are called to be builders, creating spaces and relationships that reflect God's love, justice, and truth. This calling aligns with Jesus' teachings about the wise builder who built his house on the rock, symbolizing a life grounded in God's word (Matthew 7:24-27).

The Divine Builder

Hebrews 3:3-4 states, *"For Jesus has been counted worthy of more glory than Moses—as much more glory as the builder of a house has more honor than the house itself. For every house is built by someone, but the builder of all things is God."* This passage reveals a profound truth: God is the ultimate builder. He is the architect of the universe, the designer of life, and the sustainer of all creation.

God's identity as the builder emphasizes His sovereignty and creative power. From the intricate design of the cosmos to the detailed plans for the tabernacle, God's handiwork is evident. His creative acts are purposeful and intentional, reflecting His divine wisdom and love. In Genesis 1, we see God meticulously creating the world, bringing order from chaos and life from void. Each aspect of creation, from the stars to human beings, bears His mark and purpose.

As the divine builder, God also shapes lives and destinies. He forms us in our mother's womb (Psalm 139:13-16), plans our paths (Jeremiah 29:11), and works all things for our good (Romans 8:28). His building is not limited to physical structures but includes our spiritual growth and transformation. Ephesians 2:10 describes us as God's workmanship, created in Christ Jesus for good works, which God prepared beforehand for us to walk in. This highlights our role as co-laborers with God, building according to His plans and purposes.

Our Identity as Builders

Being created in God's image (Genesis 1:26-27) means we share in His creative nature and ability to build. As His children, we are called to be builders in His Kingdom, reflecting His glory through our actions and creations. This divine mandate involves using our gifts, talents, and resources to create something of eternal value.

Building is more than a physical task; it is a spiritual vocation. It requires vision, perseverance, and faith. Like Nehemiah, who rebuilt the walls of Jerusalem despite opposition (Nehemiah 4), we must be determined and steadfast. Building in the Kingdom involves overcoming obstacles, trusting in God's provision, and working diligently to fulfill His purposes.

In Matthew 16:18, Jesus says to Peter, *"And I tell you, you are Peter, and on this rock, I will build my church, and the gates of hell shall not prevail against it."* This declaration underscores our identity as builders of the Church, the body of Christ. Each believer has a unique role in this construction, contributing to the spiritual edifice through prayer, service, and witness.

Building in God's Kingdom is a divine calling that reflects our identity as His children. By understanding the biblical foundation of building, recognizing God as the ultimate builder, and embracing our role as builders, we participate in God's creative and redemptive work. Through detailed planning, perseverance, and faith, we can build lives, communities, and legacies that honor God and leave a lasting impact. As we embark on this journey, let us be inspired by the examples of Noah, Moses, and Nehemiah, trusting in God's guidance and provision every step of the way.

Categories of People and the Builder's Mentality

In the grand mosaic of humanity, people can be broadly categorized based on their orientation towards life. Understanding these categories helps us appreciate the diversity of human experience and recognize the potential for growth and transformation through a builder's mentality. The world is essentially divided into three categories: Survival Oriented, Maintenance Oriented, and Growth Oriented individuals. Additionally, people can be seen as Problem Makers, Problem Watchers, or Problem Solvers, and as History Makers or History Readers. Each of these distinctions offers profound insights into how adopting a builder's mentality can elevate individuals, communities, and societies.

1. Survival Oriented: Living for the Basics

Survival Oriented individuals are those who focus on meeting their basic needs. They are often content with having a meal and a roof over their heads, living day to day with little thought for the future beyond immediate survival. This category typically includes the labor class and those in dire economic conditions.

Biblical Perspective:

In Matthew 6:25-34, Jesus addresses the basic needs of life, urging people not to worry about what they will eat, drink, or wear. He emphasizes trust in God's provision, illustrating that even those focused on survival can find peace and assurance in God.

Example:

Consider the widow of Zarephath in 1 Kings 17:8-16. She was preparing her last meal for herself and her son, resigned to their fate. However, through her encounter with the prophet Elijah and her subsequent faith and obedience, her needs were miraculously met. Her story highlights how God's provision can transform the lives of those in survival mode, enabling them to experience His abundant blessings.

2. Maintenance Oriented: Seeking Stability

Maintenance Oriented individuals aspire for a stable and predictable life. They typically hold steady jobs, earn a fixed salary, and look forward to retirement. These individuals often value security and routine, spending their evenings with activities like watching TV or reading newspapers. Government employees often exemplify this category.

Biblical Perspective:

In 1 Timothy 6:6-10, Paul talks about the value of contentment and warns against the love of money. While stability and provision are good, he encourages believers to pursue righteousness, godliness, faith, love, endurance, and gentleness.

Example:

Joseph, who served as a steward in Potiphar's house (Genesis 39), exemplifies the Maintenance Oriented category. He managed Potiphar's household with diligence and integrity, ensuring everything ran smoothly. His faithfulness in a stable role eventually led to greater opportunities and responsibilities, showing how diligence and integrity in maintenance roles can lead to growth.

3. Growth Oriented

Growth Oriented individuals are never satisfied with the status quo. They continually seek new ways to achieve prosperity and improve their lives. These individuals are often entrepreneurs, innovators, and leaders who drive progress and change.

Biblical Perspective:

The Parable of the Talents (Matthew 25:14-30) illustrates the importance of utilizing and multiplying what God has entrusted to us. The servants who invested and grew their talents were rewarded, highlighting the value of a growth-oriented mindset.

Example:

Nehemiah is a prime example of a Growth Oriented individual. He was not content with his comfortable position in the Persian court but felt a deep burden for the ruined walls of Jerusalem. His vision, planning, and leadership resulted in the successful rebuilding of the walls, demonstrating the power of a growth-oriented mindset dedicated to God's purposes (Nehemiah 1-6).

Problem Makers, Problem Watchers, and Problem Solvers

In any society, individuals can be categorized based on how they engage with challenges and opportunities: Problem Makers, Problem Watchers, and Problem Solvers.

1. Problem Makers:

These individuals often create or exacerbate problems through negative actions or attitudes. They might be driven by selfish motives, ignorance, or a lack of accountability.

2. Problem Watchers:

Unfortunately, the majority of people fall into this category. They observe problems but do not take active steps to address them. They might feel powerless or indifferent, content to let others take the initiative.

3. Problem Solvers:

A very small fraction of individuals proactively engage with challenges, seeking solutions and making positive changes. These are the leaders and innovators who drive progress and transformation.

Biblical Perspective:

The story of David and Goliath (1 Samuel 17) exemplifies these categories. While the Israelite army (Problem Watchers) stood by in fear, David (Problem Solver) took action, trusting in God to deliver victory.

Example:

Esther, in the Book of Esther, moved from being a passive observer to a proactive problem solver. She recognized the threat to her people and took courageous steps to intercede with the king, resulting in the salvation of the Jews. Her story underscores the impact of stepping into a problem-solving role.

History Makers and History Readers

People can also be categorized as History Makers or History Readers. History Makers actively shape the course of events and leave a lasting impact, while History Readers passively observe and learn from the actions of others.

1. History Makers:

These individuals are the pioneers, leaders, and innovators who drive change and leave a legacy. They are often remembered for their significant contributions and transformative actions.

2. History Readers:

The majority of people fall into this category. They learn about and reflect on the actions of History Makers but do not actively shape events themselves.

Biblical Perspective:

In Hebrews 11, often called the "Hall of Faith," we see a list of History Makers who, through their faith and actions, shaped the course of biblical history. These include Abraham, Moses, David, and many others whose lives and actions have left a lasting legacy.

Example:

Paul the Apostle is a quintessential History Maker. His missionary journeys, church planting, and epistles have profoundly influenced Christianity. His life exemplifies dedication, sacrifice, and a relentless pursuit of God's calling, shaping the faith of generations.

Building Mentality: Transforming Lives, Communities, and the World

Adopting a builder's mentality transforms not only individuals but also communities and the world at large. Builders are driven by a vision, sustained by faith, and motivated by the desire to leave a lasting legacy. They rise above the categories of survival and maintenance, embracing growth and the challenge of solving problems and making history.

Practical Steps to Embrace a Builder's Mentality

- ✓ Be Rooted in the Word: Commit to daily prayer and Bible study, seeking God's guidance and strength to build according to His will.
- ✓ Community Involvement: Engage actively in your local church and community. Identify needs and opportunities to contribute meaningfully.

- ✓ Lifelong Learning: Pursue continuous education and skill development to enhance your ability to build effectively.
- ✓ Mentorship: Seek out mentors (My Mentor and Life Coach is Prophet Jerome Fernando) and become a guide to others if you can. Share your experiences, wisdom, and encouragement.
- ✓ Faith in Action: Step out in faith, trusting that God will provide and guide you in your building endeavors. Take practical steps to implement your vision, even when faced with challenges.

By embracing a builder's mentality, we align ourselves with God's creative and redemptive work in the world. We become partners in His Kingdom, leaving a legacy that honors Him and impacts generations to come. Let us rise to the challenge, build with purpose, and create lasting change for the glory of God.

The Honor of Building: Building vs. Buying

Why Building Holds More Honor Than Buying

Building and buying represent two fundamentally different approaches to creating and acquiring value. In our modern society, buying is often seen as more convenient and time-efficient. However, the act of building holds a special honor that buying cannot match, particularly within a biblical context.

Building something requires vision, effort, dedication, and perseverance. It is a process that involves creating from scratch, often with significant personal investment and sacrifice. When you build, you engage in a journey that not only transforms the raw materials into a finished product but also transforms you in the process. This transformation is spiritual, emotional, and intellectual, as you learn, grow, and overcome challenges.

The Bible consistently honors those who build. Proverbs 24:3-4 states*, "By wisdom a house is built, and through understanding it is established; through knowledge its rooms are filled with rare and beautiful treasures."* This verse highlights that building requires wisdom, understanding, and knowledge—qualities that reflect deep engagement and thoughtful effort.

In contrast, buying something pre-made can lack the personal connection and depth of experience that building provides. While buying can be practical and sometimes necessary, it does not carry the same sense of achievement and fulfillment. The honor in building lies in the journey and the growth it fosters.

Consider the story of King Solomon, who built the temple in Jerusalem. In 1 Kings 6, we read about the detailed planning, craftsmanship, and dedication that went into constructing this sacred space. Solomon's temple was not just a building; it was a manifestation of devotion, skill, and divine guidance. The process of building the temple required extensive resources, collaboration, and unwavering commitment to God's instructions.

Biblical Examples of Builders

The Bible is replete with examples of individuals who undertook significant building projects that had lasting impacts. These biblical builders serve as models for us, illustrating the virtues and values associated with building.

Noah and the Ark

One of the earliest examples of a biblical builder is Noah. In Genesis 6:14-22, God commands Noah to build an ark to save his family and a remnant of all living creatures from the impending flood. Building the ark was no small feat; it required precise adherence to God's detailed instructions and tremendous faith in the face of skepticism and ridicule from others.

Noah's obedience and dedication in building the ark saved humanity and preserved God's creation. His example teaches us that building with God's guidance, even when the task seems insurmountable, brings divine protection and fulfillment of God's promises.

Moses and the Tabernacle

Another profound example is Moses, who was instructed by God to build the tabernacle, a portable earthly dwelling place for God among the Israelites. The tabernacle's construction, described in detail in

Exodus 25-31, required meticulous attention to God's specifications, involving various materials, artisans, and craftsmen.

Moses' leadership in building the tabernacle highlights the importance of following divine instructions and the honor of creating a space for God's presence. The tabernacle served as a focal point for worship and communion with God, underscoring the spiritual significance of building according to God's plan.

Nehemiah and the Walls of Jerusalem

Nehemiah's story, found in the book of Nehemiah, is a compelling account of leadership, faith, and resilience. Nehemiah, a cupbearer to the Persian king, felt a divine burden to rebuild the walls of Jerusalem, which had been destroyed. Despite facing intense opposition and numerous challenges, Nehemiah organized the people, secured resources, and led the reconstruction with unwavering determination.

Nehemiah's success in rebuilding the walls in just fifty-two days (Nehemiah 6:15-16) demonstrates the power of prayer, strategic planning, and community effort. His example encourages us to undertake building projects with faith, leadership, and a clear vision, knowing that God's favor and guidance are with us.

The Importance of Legacy

Building is inherently linked to the concept of legacy. When we build something of value, we create a lasting impact that transcends our own lives. This legacy can inspire, teach, and bless future generations, contributing to the ongoing work of God's Kingdom.

Consider the legacy of King David, who, although not permitted by God to build the temple, laid the groundwork for its construction by his son Solomon. David's preparations, detailed in 1 Chronicles 22, included gathering materials, organizing labor, and instilling a vision for a house dedicated to God's name. David's legacy was not only in the physical temple but also in his unwavering dedication to God's purposes.

The apostle Paul also speaks to the importance of building a spiritual legacy. In 1 Corinthians 3:10-15, Paul describes how each person should build on the foundation of Jesus Christ with care, knowing that our works will be tested by fire. The enduring quality of our building efforts—whether they be ministries, relationships, or acts of service—reflects our faithfulness and commitment to God's calling.

Action Plans and Steps

To engage in the honor of building, it is essential to approach our projects with intentionality, faith, and practical steps grounded in Scripture.

Action Plan: Building with Vision and Purpose

- ✓ Seek God's Vision: Before embarking on any building project, it is crucial to seek God's vision and purpose. This involves prayer, meditation on Scripture, and listening for the Holy Spirit's guidance. Proverbs 16:3 advises, *"Commit to the Lord whatever you do, and he will establish your plans."*

  Step: Dedicate a period of focused prayer and fasting to seek God's direction for your building project. Journal any insights, scriptures, or impressions you receive during this time.

- ✓ Plan Diligently: Once you have a clear vision, develop a detailed plan that outlines the steps, resources, and timeline needed to accomplish your project. Proverbs 21:5 states, *"The plans of the diligent lead to profit as surely as haste leads to poverty."*

  Step: Create a project plan that includes specific goals, timelines, and resource requirements. Seek counsel from wise and experienced individuals to refine your plan.
- ✓ Build with Excellence: Commit to building with excellence, reflecting God's nature in your work. Colossians 3:23-24 encourages us, *"Whatever you do, work at it with all your heart, as working for the Lord, not for human masters."*

  Step: Establish quality standards for your project and regularly review your progress to ensure excellence. Surround yourself with skilled and dedicated team members who share your commitment.
- ✓ Overcome Challenges with Faith: Building often involves facing obstacles and opposition. Like Nehemiah, rely on prayer, strategic thinking, and resilience to overcome challenges. Nehemiah 4:14 reminds us, *"Remember the Lord, who is great and awesome, and fight for your families, your sons and your daughters, your wives and your homes."*

  Step: Develop a prayer support team to intercede for your project. Identify potential challenges and create contingency plans to address them proactively.

- ✓ Create a Lasting Legacy: Focus on creating something that will endure and impact future generations. This involves investing in people, cultivating a culture of discipleship, and ensuring that your work aligns with God's eternal purposes.
  Step: Establish mentorship and training programs to equip others to carry forward the vision. Document the lessons learned and best practices to guide future builders.

By approaching your building project with intentionality, faith, and dedication, you can create something of lasting value that honors God and blesses future generations. As you build, remember that you are participating in God's divine work, leaving a legacy that reflects His glory and purposes.

Building in the Early Stages of Life

Children as Builders: The Significance of Toys like Building Blocks and Jenga

From the earliest stages of life, children are introduced to the concept of building through toys like building blocks and Jenga. These seemingly simple playthings carry profound implications for a child's development and understanding of the world.

Building blocks are often a child's first introduction to construction. They learn how to stack, balance, and connect pieces to create structures. This activity is not just about play; it is a foundational exercise in understanding spatial relationships, developing motor skills, and fostering creativity. As children manipulate the blocks, they experiment with different configurations, learning from each attempt, success, and collapse. This iterative process of building, breaking down, and rebuilding mirrors the journey of growth and learning in life.

Jenga, a game that involves removing blocks from a tower without causing it to fall, introduces children to the concepts of strategy, patience, and precision. It teaches them about the delicate balance required in construction and the importance of each piece in maintaining the integrity of the whole. As they carefully extract and place blocks, children learn to anticipate the consequences of their actions and develop problem-solving skills.

These early experiences with building toys are more than mere play; they lay the groundwork for a deeper understanding of creation, destruction, and restoration. They instill a sense of accomplishment and the joy of seeing one's efforts result in a tangible outcome.

Building Mentality: Developing a Mindset of Building from a Young Age

The lessons learned through play can profoundly impact a child's mindset. Developing a building mentality from a young age fosters resilience, creativity, and a sense of purpose. This mindset is characterized by a willingness to take on challenges, a commitment to seeing things through, and the ability to learn from failures.

Parents and educators play a crucial role in nurturing this mentality. Encouraging children to engage in activities that require planning, effort, and perseverance helps them develop these traits. Providing opportunities for children to build, whether through physical construction, art projects, or problem-solving tasks, cultivates their ability to think critically and persist despite obstacles.

Consider the biblical story of Noah, who was tasked with building the ark. Despite the enormity of the task and the ridicule he faced, Noah demonstrated unwavering faith and perseverance. His obedience and dedication to building the ark saved his family and preserved life on earth (Genesis 6:13-22). Teaching children about Noah's story can inspire them to embrace a building mentality, understanding that great tasks often require patience, effort, and faith.

Moreover, the act of building fosters a sense of ownership and responsibility. When children see the results of their labor, they gain confidence in their abilities and learn the value of hard work. This sense of accomplishment can motivate them to take on more significant challenges as they grow older, understanding that they have the capacity to create and contribute meaningfully.

Spiritual Implications: How These Early Experiences Shape Our Spiritual Building

The early experiences of building with toys like blocks and Jenga have profound spiritual implications. They are metaphors for the spiritual building that each believer undertakes in their journey with God. The principles of construction, balance, and perseverance learned in childhood can be applied to our spiritual lives.

Building a strong spiritual foundation begins with understanding that our lives are like temples being constructed for God's glory. In 1 Corinthians 3:10-11, Paul speaks of the importance of building on a solid foundation, with Jesus Christ as the cornerstone. Just as a child learns to place the first block correctly, we must ensure that our spiritual lives are grounded in Christ. Without this firm foundation, any structure we attempt to build is vulnerable to collapse.

The process of building our spiritual lives involves continual growth and improvement. Like children learning from the collapse of their block towers, we too learn from our spiritual failures and setbacks. Each mistake becomes an opportunity to rebuild stronger and more faithfully. This is echoed in Proverbs 24:16, which says, *"For though the righteous fall seven times, they rise again."* Our spiritual journey is marked by resilience and the determination to rise again after every fall.

Furthermore, the concept of building with purpose and intention is crucial. In Ephesians 2:19-22, Paul describes believers as being built together to become a dwelling in which God lives by His Spirit. This collective building requires each individual to contribute their part, just as each block in a tower plays a role in its stability. It teaches us the importance of community and working together to achieve a common purpose.

Action Plans and Steps for Building a Strong Spiritual Foundation

To cultivate a strong spiritual foundation from an early age, it is essential to integrate practical and faith-driven activities into daily life. Here are detailed action plans and steps to help children and young believers build a strong spiritual foundation:

1. Incorporate Biblical Lessons into Daily Activities

Children learn best through stories and practical applications. Use biblical stories that emphasize building, such as Noah's ark, Nehemiah rebuilding Jerusalem's walls, and Solomon building the temple, to teach valuable lessons.

Action Step: Read these stories together and discuss the qualities these builders exhibited, such as faith, obedience, perseverance, and dedication. Create simple activities that relate to these stories, like building a small model ark or wall, to reinforce the lessons.

2. Encourage Daily Prayer and Meditation on the Word

Building a strong spiritual foundation requires regular communication with God. Encourage children to develop a habit of daily prayer and meditating on the Word

Action Step: Set aside a specific time each day for family prayer and devotion. Use age-appropriate devotionals that focus on building faith and character. Encourage children to keep a prayer journal where they can write their prayers and reflect on how God answers them.

3. Foster a Sense of Community and Service

Teach children the importance of community and serving others. Building in the Kingdom of God involves contributing to the well-being of others and working together towards common goals.

Action Step: Involve children in community service projects or church activities. Explain how their efforts help build the Kingdom of God. For example, participating in a food drive or helping clean the church can demonstrate the impact of collective efforts.

4. Model Perseverance and Resilience

Children learn by example. Show them how to persevere through challenges by modeling resilience and faith in your own life.

Action Step: Share personal stories of overcoming obstacles through faith and perseverance. When facing difficulties, demonstrate a positive attitude and reliance on God's strength. Discuss how you navigate challenges and seek God's guidance in decision-making.

5. Create Opportunities for Creative Expression

Encourage children to express their faith creatively. This can include art, music, writing, or other forms of creative expression that allow them to explore and build their spiritual identity.

Action Step: Provide materials and opportunities for creative projects that reflect their understanding of God and His teachings. For example, they can create a mural of biblical stories, write songs about their faith, or keep a faith-based journal.

6. Emphasize the Importance of a Strong Foundation

Regularly remind children that a strong foundation in Christ is crucial for their spiritual growth and stability. Use practical examples and analogies to illustrate this concept.
Action Step: Conduct a simple science experiment to demonstrate the importance of a strong foundation. For example, build a small structure on sand and another on a solid surface. Discuss how the one with a solid foundation stands firm, just like a life built on Christ.

By following these action plans and steps, you can help children and young believers build a strong spiritual foundation. These early experiences with building, whether through play or faith-based activities, shape their understanding of creation, resilience, and purpose. As they grow, they will carry these lessons into their adult lives, becoming builders in the Kingdom of God, contributing to His work, and leaving a lasting legacy.

Overcoming Opposing Forces

Challenges in Building: Identifying Common Obstacles

Building, whether it be a tangible structure, a ministry, or a personal goal, inevitably encounters obstacles. These challenges can come in various forms—external pressures, internal doubts, and spiritual opposition. Recognizing and understanding these obstacles is the first step towards overcoming them.

One of the most common challenges in building is the scarcity of resources. This can include financial constraints, lack of materials, or insufficient manpower. In the book of Nehemiah, we see how Nehemiah faced the challenge of limited resources when rebuilding the walls of Jerusalem. Despite the king's support, Nehemiah had to carefully manage the available resources, rally the people, and ensure that everyone had what they needed to work effectively (Nehemiah 2:17-18).

Another significant obstacle is opposition from others. This can take the form of criticism, sabotage, or direct conflict. Nehemiah again serves as an example, facing intense opposition from Sanballat, Tobiah, and Geshem, who mocked and threatened the work (Nehemiah 4:1-3). Nehemiah's response was to pray for strength, set up defenses, and continue working with even greater determination.

Internal struggles, such as doubt and fear, can also hinder the building process. These internal battles often arise from past failures, lack of confidence, or overwhelming pressure. Gideon experienced such doubts when God called him to lead Israel against the Midianites. Despite feeling inadequate, Gideon obeyed God's command, which led to a miraculous victory (Judges 6:14-16).

The Ease of Buying: Why Many Choose to Buy Rather Than Build

In contrast to the challenges of building, buying offers an immediate, convenient solution. The allure of buying is its simplicity and speed. It eliminates the need for long-term planning, effort, and perseverance. However, this convenience often comes at the cost of deeper fulfillment and personal growth.

Buying is a transactional process; it involves exchanging money for goods or services with minimal personal involvement. While this can be practical and necessary at times, it lacks the transformative journey that building entails. When you buy, you miss out on the opportunity to develop skills, deepen relationships, and experience the profound satisfaction that comes from creating something from scratch.

The story of the Roman centurion in Luke 7:1-10 illustrates the difference between building and buying. The centurion, though a man of significant power and wealth, chose to build a synagogue for the Jewish people. This act of building earned him great respect and honor, to the point where the Jewish elders appealed to Jesus on his behalf. They said, *"This man deserves to have you do this, because he loves our nation and has built our synagogue"* (Luke 7:4-5). The centurion's decision to build rather than buy demonstrated his commitment and earned him lasting honor.

Perseverance in Building: How to Persist Through Difficulties with Faith

Perseverance is the key to overcoming the challenges of building. It involves steadfastness, resilience, and unwavering faith. The Bible provides numerous examples of individuals who persevered through difficulties and saw their building projects come to fruition.

One of the most inspiring examples of perseverance is found in the life of Nehemiah. Despite facing numerous obstacles, Nehemiah remained committed to rebuilding the walls of Jerusalem. His strategy involved prayer, planning, and practical action. Nehemiah's response to opposition was to pray for strength, encourage the people, and implement practical measures such as setting guards and dividing the work (Nehemiah 4:9-14).

Another example is the Apostle Paul, who faced relentless persecution and hardship in his mission to build the early church. In 2 Corinthians 11:24-28, Paul recounts the many trials he endured—beatings, shipwrecks, imprisonments, and constant danger. Despite these hardships, Paul's perseverance was rooted in his faith in God's calling and his commitment to spreading the gospel. He wrote, *"Therefore, my dear brothers and sisters, stand firm. Let nothing move you. Always give yourselves fully to the work of the Lord, because you know that your labor in the Lord is not in vain" (*1 Corinthians 15:58).

Action Plans and Steps

To persevere through the difficulties of building, it is essential to develop a practical and faith-driven approach. Here are detailed action plans and steps to help you stay motivated and overcome obstacles:

1. Establish a Strong Foundation of Faith

Begin by grounding your building project in faith. Spend time in prayer, seek God's guidance, and immerse yourself in His Word. Faith is the foundation that will sustain you through challenges.

Action Step: Dedicate time each day for prayer and Bible study. Focus on scriptures that speak to God's promises, strength, and guidance. Keep a journal to document your reflections and prayers.

2. Create a Detailed Plan

Develop a comprehensive plan for your building project. Outline the vision, goals, resources needed, and potential challenges. Having a clear plan will help you stay organized and focused.

Action Step: Write a detailed project plan that includes specific goals, timelines, resource requirements, and contingency plans. Review and update your plan regularly.

3. Build a Support Network

Surround yourself with a community of supporters who can provide encouragement, advice, and assistance. This network can include family, friends, mentors, and fellow believers.

Action Step: Identify and reach out to individuals who can support your project. Create a support group that meets regularly to pray, share updates, and offer encouragement.

4. Identify Challenges: Reflect on your current building project. List the challenges you are facing or anticipate facing. Be specific and honest about the obstacles in your path.

Action Step: Develop a Strategy: Create a practical strategy to address each challenge. Include specific actions you can take, resources you need, and support you can enlist.

5. Stay Committed and Flexible

Commit to your project wholeheartedly, but remain flexible to adapt to changing circumstances. Challenges may require you to adjust your approach, but do not lose sight of your ultimate goal.

Action Step: Set short-term and long-term goals to track your progress. Celebrate small victories along the way to stay motivated. Be willing to make adjustments as needed.

6. Focus on God's Strength

Remember that your strength comes from God. When you face difficulties, lean on His power and promises. Trust that He will provide the strength and resources you need to persevere.

Action Step: Memorize key scriptures that reinforce God's strength and provision. Recite these verses during times of difficulty. Examples include Philippians 4:13 and Isaiah 41:10.

7. Reflect and Reevaluate

Periodically take time to reflect on your progress and reevaluate your approach. Assess what is working well and what needs adjustment. Seek God's guidance in making necessary changes.

Action Step: Schedule regular reflection sessions to review your project plan and progress. Use these times to pray, seek God's wisdom, and make any necessary adjustments.

By following these action plans and steps, you can navigate the challenges of building with faith and perseverance. Remember that every great work of God faces opposition, but through His strength and guidance, you can overcome and create something that honors Him and leaves a lasting legacy. As you build, you are participating in God's divine work, contributing to His Kingdom, and fulfilling His purpose for your life.

Jesus as the Master Builder

New Testament Insights: Jesus' Role as a Builder of the Church

In the New Testament, Jesus is depicted as the ultimate builder, not of physical structures but of the spiritual foundation of the Church. His entire ministry was focused on laying the groundwork for what would become the global body of believers, the Church. In Matthew 16:18, Jesus declares, *"And I tell you that you are Peter, and on this rock, I will build my church, and the gates of Hades will not overcome it."* This statement not only underscores Jesus' role as the builder of the Church but also emphasizes the 'enduring' nature of His construction.

Jesus' approach to building the Church was multifaceted. He began by selecting and training a small group of disciples, imparting to them His teachings, values, and mission. Through parables, sermons, and personal example, He laid a spiritual foundation that was strong, cohesive, and resilient. The teachings of Jesus, encapsulated in the Gospels, provided the blueprint for the early Church and continue to guide believers today.

His method was not one of haste but of careful, deliberate planning and execution. By investing in His disciples and ensuring they understood the principles of the Kingdom of God, Jesus ensured that the Church would grow organically and robustly. His ultimate sacrifice on the cross and subsequent resurrection were the capstone of His building efforts, securing salvation and eternal life for all who believe.

Ingredients of Jesus' Building: Analyze the Components that made Jesus' Building Enduring and Impactful

Jesus' approach to building the Church incorporated several key components that ensured its longevity and impact. These components can serve as a model for us as we seek to build within the Kingdom of God.

- ✓ Foundation of Truth: Jesus' teachings were rooted in the truth of God's Word. He frequently referenced Old Testament scriptures, showing their fulfillment in His life and mission. His messages were not just philosophical musings but were grounded in divine truth. For instance, in John 14:6, Jesus says, *"I am the way and the truth and the life. No one comes to the Father except through me."* This foundational truth is the bedrock of the Christian faith.
- ✓ Investment in People: Jesus dedicated significant time to His disciples, teaching them, correcting them, and preparing them for their future roles. He saw the potential in each person and invested in their development. For example, He transformed Peter from a simple fisherman into a foundational leader of the early Church. This investment in people ensured that the Church would have strong, capable leaders after His ascension.
- ✓ Empowerment through the Holy Spirit: Before His ascension, Jesus promised to send the Holy Spirit to empower His followers. In Acts 1:8, He said, *"But you will receive power when the Holy Spirit comes on you; and you will be my witnesses in Jerusalem, and in all Judea*

and Samaria, and to the ends of the earth." The Holy Spirit's presence and power were essential for the growth and expansion of the Church.

- ✓ Service and Sacrifice: Jesus' life was marked by service and sacrifice. He demonstrated servant leadership, washing His disciples' feet and teaching them to serve others humbly (John 13:1-17). His ultimate sacrifice on the cross exemplified the greatest act of love and service, providing a model for His followers to emulate.
- ✓ Community and Fellowship: Jesus fostered a sense of community among His followers. He emphasized the importance of loving one another, as seen in John 13:34-35: *"A new command I give you: Love one another. As I have loved you, so you must love one another. By this everyone will know that you are my disciples, if you love one another."* This sense of community and mutual support was crucial for the early Church and remains vital today.
- ✓ Resilience and Perseverance: Jesus prepared His followers for the challenges they would face. He warned them of persecution but also assured them of His presence and support (Matthew 10:16-22). This preparation helped the early believers remain resilient and persevere through trials.

Lessons from Jesus' Ministry: Practical Applications for Modern Builders in the Kingdom

The principles Jesus employed in building the Church provide valuable lessons for us as modern builders in the Kingdom of God. Here are some practical applications drawn from His ministry:

- ✓ Lay a Strong Foundation: Ensure that everything you build is grounded in the truth of God's Word. Study the scriptures diligently and apply their teachings to your life and work. As Jesus said in Matthew 7:24-25, *"Therefore everyone who hears these words of mine and puts them into practice is like a wise man who built his house on the rock. The rain came down, the streams rose, and the winds blew and beat against that house; yet it did not fall, because it had its foundation on the rock."*
- ✓ Invest in People: Recognize the potential in others and invest in their growth and development. Mentor, teach, and encourage those around you, helping them to realize their God-given potential. This investment will yield lasting fruit, as it did with Jesus' disciples.
- ✓ Empower through the Holy Spirit: Rely on the power of the Holy Spirit in all your decisions and endeavors. Pray for guidance, strength, and empowerment, knowing that the Spirit equips and enables you to fulfill your God-given mission.
- ✓ Serve and Sacrifice: Emulate Jesus' example of servant leadership. Seek opportunities to serve others humbly and sacrificially. By doing so, you demonstrate the love of Christ and build a community of mutual support and care.
- ✓ Foster Community and Fellowship: Build strong relationships within your community. Encourage love, support, and accountability among believers. This sense of fellowship

strengthens the body of Christ and provides a refuge in times of trouble.

✓ Prepare for Challenges: Understand that building in the Kingdom of God will involve challenges and opposition. Prepare yourself and others by fostering resilience and perseverance. Trust in God's promises and remain steadfast in your mission.

By applying these principles and action plans, you can build in the Kingdom of God with the same intentionality, care, and faithfulness that Jesus demonstrated. As you follow His example, you will contribute to the growth and strengthening of the Church, leaving a lasting legacy for future generations.

Nehemiah and the Walls of Jerusalem

The story of Nehemiah is a profound illustration of strategic building, spiritual leadership, and unwavering dedication to God's work. This Old Testament narrative provides invaluable insights into the qualities required to build effectively in the Kingdom of God. Nehemiah's journey, as recorded in the book named after him, is not just a tale of physical reconstruction but also one of spiritual restoration and communal revival.

Old Testament Example: The Story of Nehemiah as a Builder

Nehemiah was a Jewish cupbearer to the Persian King Artaxerxes. Upon hearing about the desolation of Jerusalem and the broken walls, Nehemiah was deeply grieved. His sorrow for his homeland and the plight of his people moved him to action. The first step in Nehemiah's journey was prayer. He turned to God with a heartfelt plea for guidance and favor (Nehemiah 1:4-11). This initial response of prayer set the tone for all his subsequent actions.

Nehemiah's approach to rebuilding the walls of Jerusalem was multifaceted. He began with seeking permission from King Artaxerxes, who granted him leave and provided letters of safe passage along with resources for the reconstruction (Nehemiah 2:1-8). This underscores the importance of securing the necessary support and resources before embarking on any significant project.

Upon his arrival in Jerusalem, Nehemiah didn't rush into action. Instead, he conducted a thorough inspection of the walls at night, assessing the damage and formulating a strategic plan (Nehemiah 2:11-16). This careful assessment highlights the need for understanding the scope of work and challenges before initiating the building process.

Strategic Building: The Planning and Execution of Rebuilding Jerusalem's Walls

Nehemiah's strategic approach was meticulous. He divided the work among the people, assigning specific sections of the wall to different families and groups (Nehemiah 3). This delegation of tasks not only expedited the process but also fostered a sense of community and shared responsibility. Each group's dedication to their portion of the wall ensured that the project progressed efficiently.

However, the rebuilding effort was not without opposition. Nehemiah and the people faced significant resistance from neighboring enemies, including Sanballat and Tobiah, who mocked and threatened them (Nehemiah 4:1-3). Nehemiah's response was twofold: he encouraged the people to pray and posted guards to protect the workers (Nehemiah 4:9). This dual approach of spiritual and practical defense was crucial in maintaining morale and safety.

Despite the threats, the people continued to work with a trowel in one hand and a sword in the other (Nehemiah 4:17). This vivid imagery symbolizes the balance between building and protecting, emphasizing the need for vigilance and preparedness in the face of opposition.

Nehemiah also addressed internal issues that arose, such as the exploitation of the poor by wealthy Jews. He confronted these injustices and implemented reforms to ensure fairness and unity among the people (Nehemiah 5). His leadership in resolving conflicts and promoting justice was instrumental in sustaining the community's commitment to the project.

Spiritual Leadership: Lessons from Nehemiah's Leadership and Dedication

Nehemiah's leadership was characterized by several key attributes that are essential for anyone seeking to build in the Kingdom of God.

- ✓ Prayerful Dependence on God: Throughout the entire process, Nehemiah's reliance on prayer was evident. He sought God's guidance, strength, and protection at every step. This deep spiritual foundation ensured that his actions were aligned with God's will.
- ✓ Vision and Inspiration: Nehemiah communicated a clear vision to the people, inspiring them to take on the monumental task. His ability to articulate the importance of rebuilding the walls and the spiritual significance behind it galvanized the community into action.
- ✓ Courage and Determination: Nehemiah faced significant external and internal challenges. His courage to confront these issues head-on and his unwavering determination to see the project through were critical to its success. He did not let fear or opposition deter him from his mission.
- ✓ Effective Delegation and Teamwork: By assigning specific tasks to different groups, Nehemiah ensured that the workload was manageable and that everyone felt a sense of ownership in the project. This effective delegation maximized productivity and fostered unity.

- ✓ Justice and Compassion: Nehemiah's handling of the exploitation within the community demonstrated his commitment to justice and compassion. By addressing these issues, he maintained the integrity and morale of the people.
- ✓ Resilience and Adaptability: The ability to adapt to changing circumstances and persevere through difficulties was a hallmark of Nehemiah's leadership. His resilience inspired the people to continue working despite the adversities they faced.

Practical Applications for Modern Builders in the Kingdom

The story of Nehemiah offers numerous lessons and practical applications for those looking to build in the Kingdom of God today. Here are detailed examples, action plans, and steps to engage and motivate modern builders:

Action Plan 1: Begin with Prayer

Example: Like Nehemiah, start every project with prayer. Seek God's guidance, wisdom, and favor for your endeavors.

Steps:

- ✓ Dedicate specific times each day to pray for your project.
- ✓ Involve others in prayer, forming a prayer team to support the initiative.
- ✓ Keep a prayer journal to record prayers and how God answers them, providing encouragement and testimony to His faithfulness.

Action Plan 2: Conduct Thorough Assessment

Example: Nehemiah inspected the walls before beginning the reconstruction.

Steps:

- ✓ Evaluate the current state of your project, identifying strengths, weaknesses, opportunities, and threats (SWOT analysis).
- ✓ Consult with experts and gather necessary data to understand the scope of work.
- ✓ Develop a detailed plan outlining the steps needed to achieve the project goals.

Action Plan 3: Secure Resources and Support

Example: Nehemiah sought permission and resources from King Artaxerxes.

Steps:

- ✓ Identify the resources needed for your project, including finances, materials, and personnel.
- ✓ Present your vision and plan to potential supporters, seeking their assistance.
- ✓ Establish partnerships and networks to gain additional support and resources.

Action Plan 4: Delegate Tasks and Foster Teamwork

Example: Nehemiah assigned specific sections of the wall to different groups.

Steps:

- ✓ Break down the project into manageable tasks and assign them to individuals or teams based on their strengths and expertise.
- ✓ Hold regular meetings to coordinate efforts, address challenges, and celebrate progress.
- ✓ Encourage a collaborative environment where everyone feels valued and part of the mission.

Action Plan 5: Address Challenges with Faith and Action

Example: Nehemiah prayed and posted guards in response to threats.

Steps:

- ✓ Anticipate potential challenges and develop contingency plans.
- ✓ Maintain a balance between spiritual vigilance and practical measures to address issues.
- ✓ Encourage resilience and adaptability within the team, fostering a culture of perseverance.

By applying these principles and action plans drawn from Nehemiah's example, modern builders in the Kingdom of God can undertake their projects with a solid spiritual foundation, strategic planning, and resilient leadership. Nehemiah's story serves as an enduring testament to what can be achieved when we align our efforts with God's will, remain steadfast in the face of opposition, and build with a vision that extends beyond ourselves to the greater glory of God.

The Six Ingredients of Enduring Buildings (C.E.M.E.N.T.)

In the Kingdom of God, building is not merely a physical act but a spiritual endeavor that requires careful planning and divine guidance. To create something that endures and leaves a lasting legacy, our efforts must incorporate six essential ingredients: *Continuity, Establishment, Memorial, Endure, Noble Purpose, and Timelessness.* These elements form the acronym C.E.M.E.N.T., symbolizing the strong, binding material that holds our spiritual edifices together.

1. Continuity: Ensuring Continuous Development and Growth

Continuity is about maintaining progress and ensuring that the building process does not stagnate. In spiritual terms, this means fostering an ongoing relationship with God and continuous growth in faith.

Action Plan: Steps to Maintain Continuity in Your Building Projects

- ✓ Regular Prayer and Reflection: Consistently seek God's guidance through prayer and being rooted in His Word. Establish a daily routine of devotion to stay connected with God's will for your project.
- ✓ Ongoing Education: Invest in continuous learning about God's Word. Attend Bible studies, seminars, and workshops to deepen your understanding and application of biblical principles.
- ✓ Mentorship and Discipleship: Engage with mentors (My mentor and life coach is Prophet Jerome Fernando) who can provide wisdom

and guidance. Also, disciple others, sharing the knowledge and insights you have gained.

Examples: Case Studies of Continuous Building Efforts in the Bible

The apostle Paul exemplified continuity in his ministry. Despite numerous hardships, he continuously spread the gospel, established churches, and mentored leaders (Acts 20:18-21). His letters to the churches reflect ongoing support and guidance, ensuring that the foundations he laid continued to grow and strengthen.

2. Establishment/Established: Laying a Strong Foundation

A building can only be as strong as its foundation. Establishment involves setting a solid base upon which all future work can securely rest.

Action Plan: Practical Ways to Ensure a Solid Foundation

- ✓ Biblical Principles: Ground your projects in the foundational truths of Scripture. Ensure that every aspect aligns with God's Word.
- ✓ Spiritual Disciplines: Establish a strong foundation of spiritual disciplines such as prayer, fasting, and studying the Bible. These practices fortify your spiritual base.
- ✓ Community Support: Build a supportive community that shares your vision and values. Surround yourself with people who can provide encouragement and accountability.

Examples: Biblical Examples of Strong Foundations

Jesus spoke about the importance of a strong foundation in the parable of the wise and foolish builders (Matthew 7:24-27). The wise man who built his house on the rock represents those who hear and act on Jesus' teachings, ensuring their lives are founded on solid, unshakable ground.

3. Memorial: Creating Something That Stands as a Testament

A memorial is a lasting testament that honors God and serves as a reminder of His faithfulness and provision.

Action Plan: How to Build Memorials That Honor God

- ✓ Monuments of Faith: Create physical or symbolic monuments that commemorate significant spiritual milestones. This could be as simple as a journal entry or as elaborate as a church building.
- ✓ Storytelling: Share testimonies of God's work in your life and projects. Document these stories to inspire future generations.
- ✓ Annual Celebrations: Establish annual events to remember and celebrate God's faithfulness. These events can serve as ongoing reminders of His blessings.

Examples: Memorials in the Bible That Served Significant Purposes

When the Israelites crossed the Jordan River, God commanded them to set up twelve stones as a memorial (Joshua 4:1-7). This monument served as a lasting reminder of God's miraculous provision and faithfulness, teaching future generations about His power and care.

4. Endure: Building to Withstand Time and Challenges

To endure means to build something that can withstand the tests of time and adversity. This requires resilience, steadfastness, and reliance on God's strength.

Action Plan: Strategies to Ensure Your Building Endures

- ✓ Resilience Training: Prepare for challenges by developing spiritual resilience. Study the lives of biblical figures who overcame adversity.
- ✓ Prayer for Strength: Regularly pray for God's strength and guidance to persevere through difficulties.
- ✓ Long-Term Vision: Keep a long-term perspective, focusing on the ultimate goal rather than temporary setbacks.

Examples: Biblical Structures That Endured Through Time

The temple built by Solomon is a prime example of endurance (1 Kings 6). Despite being destroyed and rebuilt, its significance endured through generations as a central place of worship and a symbol of God's presence among His people.

5. Noble Purpose: Building for a Higher Purpose

Every building project in God's Kingdom should serve a noble and higher purpose, aligning with divine intentions and contributing to the greater good.

Action Plan: Aligning Your Projects with Divine Intentions

- ✓ Purpose Statement: Clearly define the noble purpose of your project. Write a purpose statement that aligns with biblical values and goals.
- ✓ Service Orientation: Ensure that your project serves others and advances God's Kingdom.

Integrate acts of service and charity into your building efforts.

- ✓ Regular Evaluation: Continuously evaluate your project to ensure it remains aligned with its noble purpose. Make adjustments as needed to stay on course.

Examples: Projects in the Bible That Served Noble Purposes

Nehemiah's rebuilding of Jerusalem's walls served not only to protect the city but also to restore the community's faith and honor God (Nehemiah 6:15-16). His work was driven by a higher purpose, demonstrating dedication to God's glory and the well-being of His people.

6. Timelessness: Creating Timeless and Relevant Structures

Timelessness involves building something that remains relevant and valuable across generations, transcending cultural and temporal changes.

Action Plan: Ensuring Your Building Remains Relevant Across Generations

- ✓ Intergenerational Collaboration: Involve different generations in your building projects to ensure they meet the needs of all ages.
- ✓ Adaptability: Design your projects with flexibility to adapt to future changes and challenges.
- ✓ Legacy Planning: Plan for the long-term impact of your projects. Consider how they will be maintained and built upon by future generations.

Examples: Timeless Buildings and Their Impact

The Great Commission given by Jesus to His disciples (Matthew 28:18-20) is a timeless mandate.

The early church, established by the apostles, has continued to grow and adapt throughout history, demonstrating the enduring relevance of Jesus' teachings and the church's mission.

By incorporating these six ingredients—Continuity, Establishment, Memorial, Endure, Noble Purpose, and Timelessness—you can ensure that your building efforts in the Kingdom of God are enduring, impactful, and aligned with His divine will. The principles of C.E.M.E.N.T. not only provide a solid foundation for your projects but also inspire and guide you to create something of lasting value that honors God and serves His people for generations to come.

Practical Steps to Being a Builder in the Kingdom

Building in the Kingdom of God is a profound and transformative endeavor. It is a calling that requires intentionality, faith, and dedication. This chapter provides detailed, practical steps to help you identify, plan, execute, and maintain your building projects while overcoming setbacks, all grounded in the Word of God.

1. Identifying Your Building Project: Finding What God Has Called You to Build

The first step in being a builder in the Kingdom is discerning what God has called you to build. This process involves prayer, reflection, and seeking God's will.

Understanding God's Call: Begin by immersing yourself in prayer and Scripture, asking God to reveal His specific calling for you. Reflect on your passions, gifts, and the needs around you. Often, God's calling aligns with the unique talents He has given you and the burdens He has placed on your heart.

Biblical Example: Nehemiah

Nehemiah's calling to rebuild the walls of Jerusalem began with a burden. When he heard about the state of Jerusalem, he wept, prayed, and fasted (Nehemiah 1:4). God placed a specific project in Nehemiah's heart, and through prayer and reflection, Nehemiah discerned his role as a builder.

Action Plan:

- ✓ Prayer and Fasting: Dedicate time to seek God's direction. Fast and pray, asking for clarity and guidance.

- ✓ Reflect on Your Passions: List your passions and skills. Reflect on how these can be used to serve God's Kingdom.
- ✓ Seek Counsel: Talk to spiritual mentors (My mentor is Prophet Jerome Fernando) and trusted friends. Their insights can help confirm God's calling.

2. Planning and Preparation: How to Prepare for Your Building Journey

Once you have identified your building project, the next step is thorough planning and preparation. This stage is crucial to laying a solid foundation for your endeavor.

Developing a Vision: A clear vision is essential. It provides direction and motivation. Write down your vision, ensuring it aligns with biblical principles and God's calling.

Biblical Example: Moses

Before leading the Israelites out of Egypt, Moses received detailed instructions from God. He spent time in preparation, receiving the law and the blueprint for the tabernacle (Exodus 25-31). This preparation was critical for the success of his mission.

Action Plan:

- ✓ Write Your Vision: Clearly articulate your vision. Include the purpose, goals, and desired outcomes.
- ✓ Study and Research: Gather all necessary information. Study the Word of God and other relevant resources.
- ✓ Create a Plan: Develop a detailed plan outlining the steps required to achieve your

vision. Include timelines, resources needed, and potential challenges.

3. Execution and Maintenance: Practical Steps to Build and Maintain Your Project

With a vision and plan in place, it is time to execute your project. This stage requires action, dedication, and regular maintenance.

Taking Action: Begin by taking small, consistent steps. Trust in God's guidance and provision as you move forward.

Biblical Example: Solomon

When building the temple, Solomon followed the detailed plans given to him by his father, David, and God's instructions. He enlisted skilled workers, gathered materials, and ensured every aspect was meticulously executed (1 Kings 6).

Action Plan:

- ✓ Start Small: Begin with manageable tasks. This builds momentum and confidence.
- ✓ Regular Prayer: Continually seek God's guidance and wisdom. Pray for strength and perseverance.
- ✓ Monitor Progress: Regularly review your progress. Make adjustments as needed to stay on track.

Maintenance: Building in God's Kingdom requires ongoing effort to maintain and nurture what has been created.

Biblical Example: Paul

Paul's letters to the early churches were part of his ongoing effort to maintain and nurture the communities he helped establish. He provided guidance, correction, and encouragement to ensure their growth and stability (1 Corinthians, Galatians).

Action Plan:

- ✓ Regular Check-ins: Periodically assess the health and progress of your project. Make necessary adjustments.
- ✓ Seek Feedback: Engage with others involved in or impacted by your project. Their feedback can provide valuable insights.
- ✓ Continuous Improvement: Always look for ways to improve and enhance your work. Stay open to learning and growth.

4. Overcoming Setbacks: Strategies for Dealing with Challenges and Failures

Setbacks are inevitable, but with faith and perseverance, they can be overcome. The key is to remain steadfast and trust in God's plan.

Facing Challenges: Expect obstacles and be prepared to face them with resilience and trust in God.

Biblical Example: Job

Job faced immense suffering and loss, yet he remained faithful. His story teaches us about perseverance and trusting God's sovereignty even in the darkest times (Job 1-42).

Action Plan:

- ✓ Trust in God: Lean on your faith. Remember that God is in control and has a purpose for every challenge.
- ✓ Stay Resilient: Keep moving forward despite setbacks. Use them as opportunities for growth and learning.
- ✓ Seek Support: Don't face challenges alone. Reach out to your faith community for prayer and support.

Learning from Failures: Failures can be powerful learning experiences. Embrace them as part of the building process.

Biblical Example: Peter

Peter's denial of Jesus was a significant failure, yet it led to his restoration and strengthened faith. Jesus forgave and reinstated him, demonstrating that failure is not the end (John 21:15-19).

Action Plan:

- ✓ Reflect and Learn: After a failure, take time to reflect on what went wrong and what can be learned.
- ✓ Seek God's Forgiveness: If your failure involves sin or disobedience, seek God's forgiveness and grace.
- ✓ Move Forward: Apply the lessons learned and continue building. Failure is a step towards growth and improvement.

By following these practical steps, you can effectively identify, plan, execute, and maintain your building projects in the Kingdom of God. Remember that every effort, no matter how small, contributes to God's greater plan. Trust in His guidance, lean on His strength, and persevere through challenges, knowing that your work honors God and builds a lasting legacy in His Kingdom.

Examples from the Secular World of Lasting Legacies, each Demonstrating the Principles of C.E.M.E.N.T.

These examples illustrate how the principles of C.E.M.E.N.T. are embodied in various ways, leaving lasting legacies that benefit future generations.

1. **Wangari Maathai and the Green Belt Movement**
   - ✓ Continuity: Wangari Maathai started the Green Belt Movement in Kenya to combat deforestation, soil erosion, and water scarcity. The movement has planted over 51 million trees and continues to grow.
   - ✓ Establishment: She laid a strong foundation by engaging communities and empowering women to take charge of their environment.
   - ✓ Memorial: The planted forests stand as living memorials to her work.
   - ✓ Endure: The Green Belt Movement has endured beyond her lifetime, continuing her vision.
   - ✓ Noble Purpose: The movement serves the higher purpose of environmental conservation and community empowerment.
   - ✓ Timelessness: The forests planted will benefit future generations, ensuring her legacy remains relevant.

2. **Marie Curie and Advancements in Science**

- ✓ Continuity: Marie Curie's groundbreaking research in radioactivity laid the groundwork for future scientific advancements.
- ✓ Establishment: She established new scientific fields and methodologies.
- ✓ Memorial: Her discoveries are memorialized in the periodic table and numerous scientific institutions.
- ✓ Endure: Her work endures in modern medicine and technology.
- ✓ Noble Purpose: Curie's research aimed at improving human health and knowledge.
- ✓ Timelessness: Her contributions continue to influence science and medicine.

3. Martin Luther King Jr. and the Civil Rights Movement

- ✓ Continuity: MLK's leadership in the Civil Rights Movement set the stage for ongoing efforts toward equality.
- ✓ Establishment: He established a foundation of nonviolent resistance and powerful oratory.
- ✓ Memorial: Monuments and a national holiday honor his legacy.
- ✓ Endure: His speeches and writings continue to inspire movements for justice.
- ✓ Noble Purpose: His purpose was to achieve civil rights and social justice.
- ✓ Timelessness: His message remains relevant to ongoing struggles for equality.

4. John Muir and National Parks

- ✓ Continuity: John Muir's advocacy led to the creation of national parks in the U.S.

- ✓ Establishment: He helped establish the National Park Service.
- ✓ Memorial: Parks like Yosemite serve as memorials to his conservation efforts.
- ✓ Endure: National parks continue to protect natural landscapes.
- ✓ Noble Purpose: Muir's purpose was to preserve nature for all to enjoy.
- ✓ Timelessness: The parks offer timeless beauty and environmental preservation.

5. Mother Teresa and Missionaries of Charity

- ✓ Continuity: Mother Teresa founded the Missionaries of Charity, which continues her work worldwide.
- ✓ Establishment: She established a network of care for the poor and sick.
- ✓ Memorial: Her work is memorialized in the institutions she founded.
- ✓ Endure: The Missionaries of Charity continue to operate globally.
- ✓ Noble Purpose: Her purpose was to serve the least fortunate.
- ✓ Timelessness: Her legacy of compassion endures in every act of service performed by her order.

6. Norman Borlaug and the Green Revolution

- ✓ Continuity: Norman Borlaug's agricultural innovations sparked the Green Revolution.
- ✓ Establishment: He established high-yield crop varieties and farming techniques.
- ✓ Memorial: His legacy is seen in the fields that produce abundant food.

- ✓ Endure: His contributions continue to feed billions.
- ✓ Noble Purpose: Borlaug aimed to alleviate hunger.
- ✓ Timelessness: His impact on global food security remains critical.

7. Jane Goodall and Primate Research

- ✓ Continuity: Jane Goodall's research on chimpanzees continues through the Jane Goodall Institute.
- ✓ Establishment: She established long-term studies of primates.
- ✓ Memorial: The institute and research sites serve as memorials.
- ✓ Endure: Her work endures in ongoing research and conservation efforts.
- ✓ Noble Purpose: Her purpose was to understand and protect primates.
- ✓ Timelessness: Her findings continue to shape primate conservation.

8. Bill Gates and Philanthropy

- ✓ Continuity: Bill Gates' philanthropic efforts continue through the Bill & Melinda Gates Foundation.
- ✓ Establishment: He established a foundation focusing on global health and education.
- ✓ Memorial: The foundation's work serves as a living memorial.
- ✓ Endure: The foundation's initiatives continue to impact lives.
- ✓ Noble Purpose: His purpose is to improve global well-being.

- ✓ Timelessness: The foundation's work will have long-lasting effects.

9. Fred Rogers and Educational Television

- ✓ Continuity: Fred Rogers created "Mister Rogers' Neighborhood," which continues to educate and comfort children.
- ✓ Establishment: He established a new genre of educational television.
- ✓ Memorial: His show and related media serve as memorials.
- ✓ Endure: The show's lessons endure through syndication and digital media.
- ✓ Noble Purpose: His purpose was to educate and nurture children.
- ✓ Timelessness: The timeless values he taught remain relevant.

10. Rosa Parks and Civil Rights Activism

- ✓ Continuity: Rosa Parks' act of defiance sparked the Montgomery Bus Boycott and the Civil Rights Movement.
- ✓ Establishment: She helped establish the momentum for systemic change.
- ✓ Memorial: Her legacy is honored through numerous awards and remembrances.
- ✓ Endure: The movement she helped catalyze endures in ongoing civil rights work.
- ✓ Noble Purpose: Her purpose was to challenge racial injustice.
- ✓ Timelessness: Her bravery continues to inspire activists.

Examples of Builders in the Kingdom

Old Testament Example: King Solomon
King Solomon, the son of King David, is a quintessential example of a builder in the Kingdom of God. Solomon is renowned for constructing the First Temple in Jerusalem, a monumental achievement that fulfilled the promise God made to his father, David. This Temple became the center of worship and the symbol of God's presence among His people. Solomon's dedication to building the Temple, despite the immense resources and effort required, reflects his deep commitment to God and his understanding of the importance of creating a sacred space for worship. His wisdom, granted by God, enabled him to lead Israel into a period of unprecedented peace and prosperity, solidifying his legacy as a wise and effective leader and builder.

Scriptural Reference: 1 Kings 6:14 – *"So Solomon built the temple and completed it."*

New Testament Example: Apostle Paul
Apostle Paul, originally known as Saul of Tarsus, was a pivotal figure in the spread of Christianity. His missionary journeys and extensive writings laid the foundation for the early Christian Church. Paul built numerous congregations across the Roman Empire, tirelessly teaching and encouraging new believers. His letters, which form a significant portion of the New Testament, provided theological foundations, practical advice, and spiritual encouragement that continue to influence Christians today. Paul's

unwavering dedication, even in the face of persecution and imprisonment, exemplifies his role as a builder in God's Kingdom, establishing and nurturing the spiritual growth of countless individuals and communities.

Scriptural Reference: 1 Corinthians 3:10 – *"By the grace God has given me, I laid a foundation as a wise builder, and someone else is building on it. But each one should build with care."*

Secular World Example: Mother Teresa
Mother Teresa, known for her selfless service to the poor and sick in Calcutta, India, stands out as a builder in the secular world whose work was deeply rooted in her faith. She founded the Missionaries of Charity, a religious congregation that provides care for those suffering from poverty, illness, and neglect. Mother Teresa's compassion and dedication to serving the least privileged reflected the teachings of Christ and left an indelible impact on the world. Her legacy continues through the ongoing work of the Missionaries of Charity, which operates in over 130 countries, embodying her commitment to love and care for the needy.

Scriptural Reference: Matthew 25:40 – *"The King will reply, 'Truly I tell you, whatever you did for one of the least of these brothers and sisters of mine, you did for me.'"*

Personal Example: Authoring and Publishing 175 plus Books (as of Mar 2025)
As an author of 175 books, I have dedicated my life to building a lasting legacy through the written word,

with a primary focus on solving problems and providing solutions that can benefit others. My journey in writing began as a way to transfer knowledge and wisdom for future generations, ensuring that the insights and experiences God has blessed me with can continue to inspire and educate. This endeavor was not only a response to personal and community needs but also a way to make effective use of the knowledge, wisdom, time, and grace that the Lord has empowered me with.

Writing has allowed me to address various issues, offering practical guidance to management and leaders and spiritual insights to help individuals navigate their challenges. This commitment to being a solution provider has enhanced my credibility, opened new doors, and provided a continuous source of revenue, especially during times when my primary business as a trainer faced challenges, such as during the COVID-19 pandemic. Beyond financial benefits, authoring books has enabled me to provide value to people's lives, contribute positively to society, and keep my mind focused on productive and meaningful pursuits.

My family and future generations will benefit from the sale and royalties of these books, ensuring that my legacy endures long after I am gone. Every book purchased represents an opportunity for someone to gain insight and find solutions to their problems, thereby extending the impact of my work far and wide.

Scriptural Reference: Proverbs 4:7 – *"Wisdom is the principal thing; therefore get wisdom: and with all thy getting get understanding."*

Here's Why I Write Books:

- ✓ *To transfer knowledge for future generations and leave a lasting legacy.*
- ✓ *To address and provide solutions to real-life problems.*
- ✓ *To make effective use of the knowledge, wisdom, time, and grace that the Lord has empowered me with.*
- ✓ *To enhance credibility and open more professional doors.*
- ✓ *To create a second stream of income, especially useful during low periods in my training business.*
- ✓ *To ensure a continuous flow of revenue even when active work is no longer possible.*
- ✓ *To better finance Kingdom work.*
- ✓ *To benefit my family and future generations from book sales and royalties.*
- ✓ *To leave a positive legacy even after I am no longer around.*
- ✓ *To provide value to people's lives.*
- ✓ *To keep my mind occupied and away from unnecessary trouble, gossip, and other distractions.*

Decrees and Declarations for Various Aspects of Building in Life

These declarations and Bible verses are designed to help you affirm your identity as a builder in various aspects of your life. They can be used in your daily prayers, journaling, or spoken aloud as affirmations. Remember to personalize them to fit your unique circumstances and needs.

Personal Spiritual Growth, Maturity, and Development

1. *I am a builder of my faith in Christ. "So then faith comes by hearing, and hearing by the word of God." (Romans 10:17)*
   I declare that my faith is growing stronger every day as I immerse myself in the Word of God.
2. *I am a builder of my spiritual maturity. "I grow in the grace and knowledge of our Lord and Savior Jesus Christ. To Him be glory both now and forever! Amen." (2 Peter 3:18)*
   I declare that I am maturing in my walk with Christ, growing in grace and knowledge.
3. *I am a builder of my prayer life. "I pray without ceasing." (1 Thessalonians 5:17)*
   I declare that my life is marked by constant and fervent prayer.
4. *I am a builder of my spiritual strength. "I can do all things through Christ who strengthens me." (Philippians 4:13)*

I declare that I am strong and capable through Christ who empowers me.

5. *I am a builder of my spiritual discipline. "I discipline my body and bring it into subjection, lest, when I have preached to others, I myself should become disqualified." (1 Corinthians 9:27)*
   I declare that I am disciplined and self-controlled, keeping my body and spirit in alignment with God's will.
6. *I am a builder of my relationship with God. "I draw near to God, and He will draw near to me." (James 4:8)*
   I declare that my relationship with God is deepening as I draw closer to Him.
7. *I am a builder of my spiritual understanding. "Open my eyes, that I may see wondrous things from Your law." (Psalm 119:18)*
   I declare that my eyes are opened to the wonders of God's Word, increasing my understanding.
8. *I am a builder of my spiritual gifts. "I stir up the gift of God which is in me." (2 Timothy 1:6)*
   I declare that I am actively using and developing the spiritual gifts God has given me.
9. *I am a builder of my spiritual joy. "The joy of the Lord is my strength." (Nehemiah 8:10)*
   I declare that my life is filled with the joy of the Lord, which strengthens me.
10. *I am a builder of my spiritual peace. "And the peace of God, which surpasses all understanding, guards my heart and mind through Christ Jesus." (Philippians 4:7)*

I declare that God's peace, which surpasses all understanding, guards my heart and mind.

11. *I am a builder of my spiritual love. "Beloved, let us love one another, for love is of God; and everyone who loves is born of God and knows God." (1 John 4:7)*
    I declare that my life is marked by love, for I am born of God and know Him.
12. *I am a builder of my spiritual patience. "But let patience have its perfect work, that I may be perfect and complete, lacking nothing." (James 1:4)*
    I declare that patience is working in me, making me perfect and complete.
13. *I am a builder of my spiritual kindness. "And be kind to one another, tenderhearted, forgiving one another, even as God in Christ forgave you." (Ephesians 4:32)*
    I declare that I am kind, tenderhearted, and forgiving, just as God in Christ forgave me.
14. *I am a builder of my spiritual goodness. "Surely goodness and mercy shall follow me all the days of my life; And I will dwell in the house of the Lord forever." (Psalm 23:6)*
    I declare that goodness and mercy follow me all the days of my life.
15. *I am a builder of my spiritual faithfulness. "Moreover it is required in stewards that one be found faithful." (1 Corinthians 4:2)*
    I declare that I am a faithful steward of all that God has entrusted to me.
16. *I am a builder of my spiritual gentleness. "Let your gentleness be known to all men. The Lord is at hand." (Philippians 4:5)*

I declare that my gentleness is evident to all, for the Lord is near.

17. *I am a builder of my spiritual self-control. "But the fruit of the Spirit is love, joy, peace, longsuffering, kindness, goodness, faithfulness, gentleness, self-control. Against such there is no law." (Galatians 5:22-23)*
    I declare that I exhibit the fruit of the Spirit, including self-control.
18. *I am a builder of my spiritual resilience. "We are hard-pressed on every side, yet not crushed; we are perplexed, but not in despair." (2 Corinthians 4:8)*
    I declare that I am resilient, able to withstand pressure without despair.
19. *I am a builder of my spiritual perseverance. "And let us not grow weary while doing good, for in due season we shall reap if we do not lose heart." (Galatians 6:9)*
    I declare that I will not grow weary in doing good, for I will reap a harvest in due time.
20. *I am a builder of my spiritual humility. "Humble yourselves in the sight of the Lord, and He will lift you up." (James 4:10)*
    I declare that I walk in humility, and the Lord lifts me up.
21. *I am a builder of my spiritual boldness. "The wicked flee when no one pursues, but the righteous are bold as a lion." (Proverbs 28:1)*
    I declare that I am bold as a lion, for I am righteous in Christ.
22. *I am a builder of my spiritual hope. "Now may the God of hope fill you with all joy and peace in believing, that you may abound in hope by the power of the Holy Spirit." (Romans 15:13)*

I declare that I abound in hope by the power of the Holy Spirit.

23. *I am a builder of my spiritual unity with others. "Behold, how good and how pleasant it is for brethren to dwell together in unity!" (Psalm 133:1)*
    I declare that I live in unity with my brothers and sisters in Christ.
24. *I am a builder of my spiritual witness. "But you shall receive power when the Holy Spirit has come upon you; and you shall be witnesses to Me in Jerusalem, and in all Judea and Samaria, and to the end of the earth." (Acts 1:8)*
    I declare that I am a powerful witness for Christ, filled with the Holy Spirit.
25. *I am a builder of my spiritual obedience. "If you love Me, keep My commandments." (John 14:15)*
    I declare that I show my love for God by keeping His commandments.
26. *I am a builder of my spiritual courage. "Have I not commanded you? Be strong and of good courage; do not be afraid, nor be dismayed, for the Lord your God is with you wherever you go." (Joshua 1:9)*
    I declare that I am strong and courageous, for the Lord my God is with me wherever I go.
27. *I am a builder of my spiritual gratitude. "In everything give thanks; for this is the will of God in Christ Jesus for you." (1 Thessalonians 5:18)*
    I declare that I give thanks in all circumstances, for this is God's will for me.

28. *I am a builder of my spiritual generosity. "Give, and it will be given to you: good measure, pressed down, shaken together, and running over will be put into your bosom. For with the same measure that you use, it will be measured back to you." (Luke 6:38)*
    I declare that I am generous, and I receive abundantly in return.
29. *I am a builder of my spiritual forgiveness. "And whenever you stand praying, if you have anything against anyone, forgive him, that your Father in heaven may also forgive you your trespasses." (Mark 11:25)*
    I declare that I forgive others, and my Father in heaven forgives me.
30. *I am a builder of my spiritual compassion. "But when He saw the multitudes, He was moved with compassion for them, because they were weary and scattered, like sheep having no shepherd." (Matthew 9:36)*
    I declare that I am moved with compassion for others, just as Jesus was.
31. *I am a builder of my spiritual devotion. "And they continued steadfastly in the apostles' doctrine and fellowship, in the breaking of bread, and in prayers." (Acts 2:42)*
    I declare that I am devoted to the teachings of the apostles, fellowship, breaking of bread, and prayer.

Christ-Confidence and Christ-Esteem

1. *I am a builder of my confidence in Christ. "I can do all things through Christ who strengthens me." (Philippians 4:13)*

I declare that I am confident in my abilities through Christ who empowers me.

2. *I am a builder of my identity in Christ. "Therefore, if anyone is in Christ, he is a new creation; old things have passed away; behold, all things have become new." (2 Corinthians 5:17)*
   I declare that I am a new creation in Christ, and my old self has passed away.
3. *I am a builder of my worth in Christ. "But you are a chosen generation, a royal priesthood, a holy nation, His own special people, that you may proclaim the praises of Him who called you out of darkness into His marvelous light." (1 Peter 2:9)*
   I declare that I am chosen, royal, and special in God's eyes.
4. *I am a builder of my boldness in Christ. "In whom we have boldness and access with confidence through faith in Him." (Ephesians 3:12)*
   I declare that I have boldness and access to God with confidence through faith in Christ.
5. *I am a builder of my self-esteem in Christ. "I am fearfully and wonderfully made; Marvelous are Your works, And that my soul knows very well." (Psalm 139:14)*
   I declare that I am fearfully and wonderfully made by God.
6. *I am a builder of my strength in Christ. "The Lord is my strength and my shield; My heart trusted in Him, and I am helped; Therefore my heart greatly rejoices, And with my song I will praise Him." (Psalm 28:7)*

I declare that the Lord is my strength and shield, and I trust in Him.

7. *I am a builder of my victory in Christ. "Yet in all these things we are more than conquerors through Him who loved us." (Romans 8:37)*
   I declare that I am more than a conqueror through Christ who loves me.
8. *I am a builder of my purpose in Christ. "For I know the thoughts that I think toward you, says the Lord, thoughts of peace and not of evil, to give you a future and a hope." (Jeremiah 29:11)*
   I declare that God has a plan and purpose for my life, to give me a future and a hope.
9. *I am a builder of my joy in Christ. "These things I have spoken to you, that My joy may remain in you, and that your joy may be full." (John 15:11)*
   I declare that the joy of Christ remains in me, and my joy is full.
10. *I am a builder of my peace in Christ. "Peace I leave with you, My peace I give to you; not as the world gives do I give to you. Let not your heart be troubled, neither let it be afraid." (John 14:27)*
    I declare that I have the peace of Christ, and my heart is not troubled or afraid.
11. *I am a builder of my trust in Christ. "Trust in the Lord with all your heart, And lean not on your own understanding; In all your ways acknowledge Him, And He shall direct your paths." (Proverbs 3:5-6)*
    I declare that I trust in the Lord with all my heart, and He directs my paths.

12. I am a builder of my love in Christ. "And we have known and believed the love that God has for us. God is love, and he who abides in love abides in God, and God in him." (1 John 4:16)
I declare that I abide in God's love, and He abides in me.

13. I am a builder of my faith in Christ. "Now faith is the substance of things hoped for, the evidence of things not seen." (Hebrews 11:1)
I declare that my faith is strong, providing substance and evidence for what I hope for.

14. I am a builder of my perseverance in Christ. "And let us not grow weary while doing good, for in due season we shall reap if we do not lose heart." (Galatians 6:9)
I declare that I will not grow weary in doing good, for I will reap a harvest in due season.

15. I am a builder of my humility in Christ. "Humble yourselves in the sight of the Lord, and He will lift you up." (James 4:10)
I declare that I walk in humility, and the Lord lifts me up.

16. I am a builder of my hope in Christ. "Now may the God of hope fill you with all joy and peace in believing, that you may abound in hope by the power of the Holy Spirit." (Romans 15:13)
I declare that I abound in hope by the power of the Holy Spirit.

17. I am a builder of my unity in Christ. "Behold, how good and how pleasant it is for brethren to dwell together in unity!" (Psalm 133:1)
I declare that I live in unity with my brothers and sisters in Christ.

18. I am a builder of my witness in Christ. "But you shall receive power when the Holy Spirit has come upon you; and you shall be witnesses to Me in Jerusalem, and in all Judea and Samaria, and to the end of the earth." (Acts 1:8)
I declare that I am a powerful witness for Christ, filled with the Holy Spirit.

19. I am a builder of my obedience in Christ. "If you love Me, keep My commandments." (John 14:15)
I declare that I show my love for God by keeping His commandments.

20. I am a builder of my courage in Christ. "Have I not commanded you? Be strong and of good courage; do not be afraid, nor be dismayed, for the Lord your God is with you wherever you go." (Joshua 1:9)
I declare that I am strong and courageous, for the Lord my God is with me wherever I go.

21. I am a builder of my gratitude in Christ. "In everything give thanks; for this is the will of God in Christ Jesus for you." (1 Thessalonians 5:18)
I declare that I give thanks in all circumstances, for this is God's will for me.

22. I am a builder of my generosity in Christ. "Give, and it will be given to you: good measure, pressed down, shaken together, and running over will be put into your bosom. For with the same measure that you use, it will be measured back to you." (Luke 6:38)
I declare that I am generous, and I receive abundantly in return.

23. *I am a builder of my forgiveness in Christ. "And whenever you stand praying, if you have anything against anyone, forgive him, that your Father in heaven may also forgive you your trespasses." (Mark 11:25)*
    I declare that I forgive others, and my Father in heaven forgives me.
24. *I am a builder of my compassion in Christ. "But when He saw the multitudes, He was moved with compassion for them, because they were weary and scattered, like sheep having no shepherd." (Matthew 9:36)*
    I declare that I am moved with compassion for others, just as Jesus was.
25. *I am a builder of my devotion in Christ. "And they continued steadfastly in the apostles' doctrine and fellowship, in the breaking of bread, and in prayers." (Acts 2:42)*
    I declare that I am devoted to the teachings of the apostles, fellowship, breaking of bread, and prayer.
26. *I am a builder of my faithfulness in Christ. "Moreover it is required in stewards that one be found faithful." (1 Corinthians 4:2)*
    I declare that I am a faithful steward of all that God has entrusted to me.
27. *I am a builder of my perseverance in Christ. "And let us not grow weary while doing good, for in due season we shall reap if we do not lose heart." (Galatians 6:9)*
    I declare that I will not grow weary in doing good, for I will reap a harvest in due season.
28. *I am a builder of my humility in Christ. "Humble yourselves in the sight of the Lord, and He will lift you up." (James 4:10)*

I declare that I walk in humility, and the Lord lifts me up.

29. *I am a builder of my boldness in Christ. "The wicked flee when no one pursues, but the righteous are bold as a lion." (Proverbs 28:1)*
    I declare that I am bold as a lion, for I am righteous in Christ.
30. *I am a builder of my resilience in Christ. "We are hard-pressed on every side, yet not crushed; we are perplexed, but not in despair." (2 Corinthians 4:8)*
    I declare that I am resilient, able to withstand pressure without despair.
31. *I am a builder of my endurance in Christ. "But those who wait on the Lord shall renew their strength; They shall mount up with wings like eagles, They shall run and not be weary, They shall walk and not faint." (Isaiah 40:31)*
    I declare that my strength is renewed as I wait on the Lord, enabling me to run and not be weary, to walk and not faint.

Healthy Living and Wellness

1. *I am a builder of my health in Christ. "Beloved, I pray that you may prosper in all things and be in health, just as your soul prospers." (3 John 1:2)*
   I declare that I prosper in all things and am in good health as my soul prospers.
2. *I am a builder of my body's temple in Christ. "Do you not know that your body is the temple of the Holy Spirit who is in you, whom you have from God, and you are not your own?" (1 Corinthians 6:19)*

I declare that my body is the temple of the Holy Spirit, and I honor God with it.

3. *I am a builder of my strength in Christ. "I can do all things through Christ who strengthens me." (Philippians 4:13)*
   I declare that I can do all things through Christ who strengthens me.
4. *I am a builder of my endurance in Christ. "But those who wait on the Lord shall renew their strength; They shall mount up with wings like eagles, They shall run and not be weary, They shall walk and not faint." (Isaiah 40:31)*
   I declare that my strength is renewed as I wait on the Lord, enabling me to run and not be weary, to walk and not faint.
5. *I am a builder of my nourishment in Christ. "Man shall not live by bread alone, but by every word that proceeds from the mouth of God." (Matthew 4:4)*
   I declare that I am nourished by every word that comes from the mouth of God.
6. *I am a builder of my healing in Christ. "But He was wounded for our transgressions, He was bruised for our iniquities; The chastisement for our peace was upon Him, And by His stripes we are healed." (Isaiah 53:5)*
   I declare that by the stripes of Jesus, I am healed.
7. *I am a builder of my vitality in Christ. "The Lord is my strength and my song, and He has become my salvation." (Psalm 118:14)*
   I declare that the Lord is my strength and my song, and He gives me vitality.
8. *I am a builder of my rest in Christ. "Come to Me, all you who labor and are heavy laden,*

and I will give you rest." (Matthew 11:28)
I declare that I come to Jesus, and He gives me rest.

9. *I am a builder of my self-control in Christ. "For God has not given us a spirit of fear, but of power and of love and of a sound mind." (2 Timothy 1:7)*
   I declare that I have a sound mind and self-control, given by God.
10. *I am a builder of my joy in Christ. "These things I have spoken to you, that My joy may remain in you, and that your joy may be full." (John 15:11)*
    I declare that the joy of Christ remains in me, and my joy is full.
11. *I am a builder of my peace in Christ. "Peace I leave with you, My peace I give to you; not as the world gives do I give to you. Let not your heart be troubled, neither let it be afraid." (John 14:27)*
    I declare that I have the peace of Christ, and my heart is not troubled or afraid.
12. *I am a builder of my habits in Christ. "And do not be conformed to this world, but be transformed by the renewing of your mind, that you may prove what is that good and acceptable and perfect will of God." (Romans 12:2)*
    I declare that I am transformed by the renewing of my mind, proving God's perfect will.
13. *I am a builder of my confidence in Christ. "Being confident of this very thing, that He who has begun a good work in you will complete it until the day of Jesus Christ."*

(Philippians 1:6)
I declare that I am confident that God, who began a good work in me, will complete it.

14. *I am a builder of my patience in Christ. "But let patience have its perfect work, that you may be perfect and complete, lacking nothing." (James 1:4)*
    I declare that patience has its perfect work in me, making me perfect and complete.
15. *I am a builder of my discipline in Christ. "No discipline seems pleasant at the time, but painful. Later on, however, it produces a harvest of righteousness and peace for those who have been trained by it." (Hebrews 12:11)*
    I declare that discipline produces a harvest of righteousness and peace in my life.
16. *I am a builder of my stewardship in Christ. "Moreover it is required in stewards that one be found faithful." (1 Corinthians 4:2)*
    I declare that I am a faithful steward of all that God has entrusted to me.
17. *I am a builder of my generosity in Christ. "Give, and it will be given to you: good measure, pressed down, shaken together, and running over will be put into your bosom. For with the same measure that you use, it will be measured back to you." (Luke 6:38)*
    I declare that I am generous, and I receive abundantly in return.
18. *I am a builder of my gratitude in Christ. "In everything give thanks; for this is the will of God in Christ Jesus for you." (1 Thessalonians 5:18)*
    I declare that I give thanks in all circumstances, for this is God's will for me.

19. I am a builder of my relationships in Christ. "A friend loves at all times, and a brother is born for adversity." (Proverbs 17:17)
I declare that I cultivate loving and supportive relationships.

20. I am a builder of my forgiveness in Christ. "And whenever you stand praying, if you have anything against anyone, forgive him, that your Father in heaven may also forgive you your trespasses." (Mark 11:25)
I declare that I forgive others, and my Father in heaven forgives me.

21. I am a builder of my resilience in Christ. "We are hard-pressed on every side, yet not crushed; we are perplexed, but not in despair." (2 Corinthians 4:8)
I declare that I am resilient, able to withstand pressure without despair.

22. I am a builder of my endurance in Christ. "But those who wait on the Lord shall renew their strength; They shall mount up with wings like eagles, They shall run and not be weary, They shall walk and not faint." (Isaiah 40:31)
I declare that my strength is renewed as I wait on the Lord, enabling me to run and not be weary, to walk and not faint.

23. I am a builder of my vitality in Christ. "The Lord is my strength and my song, and He has become my salvation." (Psalm 118:14)
I declare that the Lord is my strength and my song, and He gives me vitality.

24. I am a builder of my hope in Christ. "Now may the God of hope fill you with all joy and peace in believing, that you may abound in hope by the power of the Holy Spirit." (Romans 15:13)

I declare that I abound in hope by the power of the Holy Spirit.

25. *I am a builder of my humility in Christ. "Humble yourselves in the sight of the Lord, and He will lift you up." (James 4:10)*
    I declare that I walk in humility, and the Lord lifts me up.
26. *I am a builder of my boldness in Christ. "The wicked flee when no one pursues, but the righteous are bold as a lion." (Proverbs 28:1)*
    I declare that I am bold as a lion, for I am righteous in Christ.
27. *I am a builder of my perseverance in Christ. "And let us not grow weary while doing good, for in due season we shall reap if we do not lose heart." (Galatians 6:9)*
    I declare that I will not grow weary in doing good, for I will reap a harvest in due season.
28. *I am a builder of my trust in Christ. "Trust in the Lord with all your heart, And lean not on your own understanding; In all your ways acknowledge Him, And He shall direct your paths." (Proverbs 3:5-6)*
    I declare that I trust in the Lord with all my heart, and He directs my paths.
29. *I am a builder of my endurance in Christ. "Blessed is the man who endures temptation; for when he has been approved, he will receive the crown of life which the Lord has promised to those who love Him." (James 1:12)*
    I declare that I endure temptation and receive the crown of life promised by the Lord.
30. *I am a builder of my self-discipline in Christ. "But I discipline my body and bring it into*

subjection, lest, when I have preached to others, I myself should become disqualified." (1 Corinthians 9:27)
I declare that I discipline my body and bring it into subjection, living a life of integrity.

31. *I am a builder of my perseverance in Christ. "Therefore, my beloved brethren, be steadfast, immovable, always abounding in the work of the Lord, knowing that your labor is not in vain in the Lord." (1 Corinthians 15:58)*
I declare that I am steadfast and immovable, always abounding in the work of the Lord.

Marriage and Relationships

1. *I am a builder of love in my marriage. "And above all these put on love, which binds everything together in perfect harmony." (Colossians 3:14)*
I declare that I put on love, binding my marriage in perfect harmony.
2. *I am a builder of unity in my marriage. "Therefore what God has joined together, let no one separate." (Mark 10:9)*
I declare that my marriage is united by God, and nothing shall separate us.
3. *I am a builder of faithfulness in my marriage. "Let marriage be held in honor among all, and let the marriage bed be undefiled, for God will judge the sexually immoral and adulterous." (Hebrews 13:4)*
I declare that I honor my marriage, keeping it pure and faithful.
4. *I am a builder of joy in my marriage. "May your fountain be blessed, and may you rejoice*

in the wife of your youth." (Proverbs 5:18)
I declare that I rejoice in my spouse, and our marriage is blessed with joy.

5. *I am a builder of peace in my marriage. "Blessed are the peacemakers, for they will be called children of God." (Matthew 5:9)*
   I declare that I am a peacemaker, bringing peace into my marriage.
6. *I am a builder of patience in my marriage. "Be completely humble and gentle; be patient, bearing with one another in love." (Ephesians 4:2)*
   I declare that I am patient and bear with my spouse in love.
7. *I am a builder of kindness in my marriage. "Be kind to one another, tenderhearted, forgiving one another, as God in Christ forgave you." (Ephesians 4:32)*
   I declare that I am kind and tenderhearted towards my spouse.
8. *I am a builder of understanding in my marriage. "Husbands, live with your wives in an understanding way, showing honor to the woman as the weaker vessel, since they are heirs with you of the grace of life, so that your prayers may not be hindered." (1 Peter 3:7)*
   I declare that I live with my spouse in an understanding and honoring way.
9. *I am a builder of respect in my marriage. "However, let each one of you love his wife as himself, and let the wife see that she respects her husband." (Ephesians 5:33)*
   I declare that I show love and respect in my marriage.

10. *I am a builder of forgiveness in my marriage. "Bear with each other and forgive one another if any of you has a grievance against someone. Forgive as the Lord forgave you." (Colossians 3:13)*
    I declare that I forgive my spouse just as the Lord forgave me.
11. *I am a builder of communication in my marriage. "Let your conversation be always full of grace, seasoned with salt, so that you may know how to answer everyone." (Colossians 4:6)*
    I declare that my conversations with my spouse are full of grace and wisdom.
12. *I am a builder of intimacy in my marriage. "The husband should fulfill his marital duty to his wife, and likewise the wife to her husband." (1 Corinthians 7:3)*
    I declare that I fulfill my marital duties with love and intimacy.
13. *I am a builder of prayer in my marriage. "Again, I say to you, if two of you agree on earth about anything they ask, it will be done for them by my Father in heaven." (Matthew 18:19)*
    I declare that my spouse and I pray together, agreeing in faith and seeing God's answers.
14. *I am a builder of support in my marriage. "Two are better than one, because they have a good reward for their toil. For if they fall, one will lift up his fellow." (Ecclesiastes 4:9-10)*
    I declare that I support and lift up my spouse in all circumstances.
15. *I am a builder of honor in my marriage. "Love one another with brotherly affection. Outdo*

one another in showing honor." (Romans 12:10)
I declare that I outdo my spouse in showing honor and affection.

16. *I am a builder of gentleness in my marriage. "A gentle answer turns away wrath, but a harsh word stirs up anger." (Proverbs 15:1)*
I declare that my words are gentle, turning away anger and fostering peace.
17. *I am a builder of faith in my marriage. "For we live by faith, not by sight." (2 Corinthians 5:7)*
I declare that my marriage is built on faith in God's promises, not on circumstances.
18. *I am a builder of humility in my marriage. "Do nothing from selfish ambition or conceit, but in humility count others more significant than yourselves." (Philippians 2:3)*
I declare that I act in humility, considering my spouse's needs above my own.
19. *I am a builder of trust in my marriage. "The heart of her husband trusts in her, and he will have no lack of gain." (Proverbs 31:11)*
I declare that my spouse's heart trusts in me, and our marriage is fruitful.
20. *I am a builder of faithfulness in my marriage. "A faithful man will abound with blessings." (Proverbs 28:20)*
I declare that I am faithful in my marriage, and we abound with blessings.
21. *I am a builder of grace in my marriage. "But he gives more grace. Therefore it says, 'God opposes the proud but gives grace to the humble.'" (James 4:6)*
I declare that God gives us more grace as we walk in humility.

22. *I am a builder of love in my marriage. "And above all these put on love, which binds everything together in perfect harmony." (Colossians 3:14)*
    I declare that love binds my marriage in perfect harmony.
23. *I am a builder of protection in my marriage. "The Lord is my strength and my shield; in him my heart trusts, and I am helped; my heart exults, and with my song I give thanks to him." (Psalm 28:7)*
    I declare that the Lord is our shield and protector, guarding our marriage.
24. *I am a builder of joy in my marriage. "May your fountain be blessed, and may you rejoice in the wife of your youth." (Proverbs 5:18)*
    I declare that I rejoice in my spouse, and our marriage is blessed with joy.
25. *I am a builder of peace in my marriage. "Blessed are the peacemakers, for they will be called children of God." (Matthew 5:9)*
    I declare that I am a peacemaker, bringing peace into my marriage.
26. *I am a builder of patience in my marriage. "Be completely humble and gentle; be patient, bearing with one another in love." (Ephesians 4:2)*
    I declare that I am patient and bear with my spouse in love.
27. *I am a builder of kindness in my marriage. "Be kind to one another, tenderhearted, forgiving one another, as God in Christ forgave you." (Ephesians 4:32)*
    I declare that I am kind and tenderhearted towards my spouse.

28. *I am a builder of understanding in my marriage. "Husbands, live with your wives in an understanding way, showing honor to the woman as the weaker vessel, since they are heirs with you of the grace of life, so that your prayers may not be hindered." (1 Peter 3:7)*
    I declare that I live with my spouse in an understanding and honoring way.
29. *I am a builder of respect in my marriage. "However, let each one of you love his wife as himself, and let the wife see that she respects her husband." (Ephesians 5:33)*
    I declare that I show love and respect in my marriage.
30. *I am a builder of forgiveness in my marriage. "Bear with each other and forgive one another if any of you has a grievance against someone. Forgive as the Lord forgave you." (Colossians 3:13)*
    I declare that I forgive my spouse just as the Lord forgave me.
31. *I am a builder of communication in my marriage. "Let your conversation be always full of grace, seasoned with salt, so that you may know how to answer everyone." (Colossians 4:6)*
    I declare that my conversations with my spouse are full of grace and wisdom.

Children, Grandchildren, and Beyond

1. *I am a builder of faith in my children. "Train up a child in the way he should go, and when he is old he will not depart from it." (Proverbs 22:6)*
   I declare that I train my children in the way

they should go, and they will not depart from it.

2. *I am a builder of love in my family. "But the greatest of these is love." (1 Corinthians 13:13)*
   I declare that love is the foundation of my family.
3. *I am a builder of wisdom in my children. "If any of you lacks wisdom, let him ask of God, who gives to all liberally and without reproach, and it will be given to him." (James 1:5)*
   I declare that my children receive wisdom from God.
4. *I am a builder of integrity in my family. "The righteous who walks in his integrity—blessed are his children after him!" (Proverbs 20:7)*
   I declare that I walk in integrity, and my children are blessed after me.
5. *I am a builder of peace in my home. "Blessed are the peacemakers, for they shall be called sons of God." (Matthew 5:9)*
   I declare that my home is a place of peace.
6. *I am a builder of joy in my family. "The joy of the Lord is your strength." (Nehemiah 8:10)*
   I declare that the joy of the Lord is our strength in my family.
7. *I am a builder of patience in my parenting. "Fathers, do not provoke your children to anger, but bring them up in the discipline and instruction of the Lord." (Ephesians 6:4)*
   I declare that I bring up my children in the discipline and instruction of the Lord.
8. *I am a builder of kindness in my family. "Be kind to one another, tenderhearted, forgiving one another, as God in Christ forgave you."*

(Ephesians 4:32)
I declare that my family is kind and tenderhearted.

9. *I am a builder of respect in my household. "Honor your father and your mother, that your days may be long in the land that the Lord your God is giving you." (Exodus 20:12)*
   I declare that respect and honor abound in my household.
10. *I am a builder of forgiveness in my family. "Forgive as the Lord forgave you." (Colossians 3:13)*
    I declare that forgiveness flows freely in my family.
11. *I am a builder of faithfulness in my family. "Let love and faithfulness never leave you; bind them around your neck, write them on the tablet of your heart." (Proverbs 3:3)*
    I declare that love and faithfulness are bound in our hearts.
12. *I am a builder of humility in my family. "Humble yourselves before the Lord, and he will lift you up." (James 4:10)*
    I declare that we humble ourselves before the Lord, and He lifts us up.
13. *I am a builder of protection over my family. "The Lord is my shepherd; I shall not want." (Psalm 23:1)*
    I declare that the Lord is our shepherd and protector.
14. *I am a builder of provision for my family. "And my God will supply every need of yours according to his riches in glory in Christ Jesus." (Philippians 4:19)*
    I declare that God supplies all our needs.

15. *I am a builder of gratitude in my family. "Give thanks in all circumstances; for this is the will of God in Christ Jesus for you." (1 Thessalonians 5:18)*
    I declare that we give thanks in all circumstances.
16. *I am a builder of strength in my family. "I can do all things through him who strengthens me." (Philippians 4:13)*
    I declare that we can do all things through Christ who strengthens us.
17. *I am a builder of hope in my family. "For I know the plans I have for you, declares the Lord, plans for welfare and not for evil, to give you a future and a hope." (Jeremiah 29:11)*
    I declare that we have a future and a hope in the Lord.
18. *I am a builder of health in my family. "Beloved, I pray that all may go well with you and that you may be in good health, as it goes well with your soul." (3 John 1:2)*
    I declare that we are in good health as it goes well with our souls.
19. *I am a builder of discipline in my family. "For the moment all discipline seems painful rather than pleasant, but later it yields the peaceful fruit of righteousness to those who have been trained by it." (Hebrews 12:11)*
    I declare that discipline in our family yields the fruit of righteousness.
20. *I am a builder of unity in my family. "How good and pleasant it is when God's people live together in unity!" (Psalm 133:1)*
    I declare that we live together in unity.

21. *I am a builder of generosity in my family. "A generous person will prosper; whoever refreshes others will be refreshed." (Proverbs 11:25)*
    I declare that we are generous and prosper in all we do.
22. *I am a builder of courage in my family. "Have I not commanded you? Be strong and courageous. Do not be frightened, and do not be dismayed, for the Lord your God is with you wherever you go." (Joshua 1:9)*
    I declare that we are strong and courageous, knowing God is with us.
23. *I am a builder of righteousness in my family. "Blessed are those who hunger and thirst for righteousness, for they shall be satisfied." (Matthew 5:6)*
    I declare that we hunger and thirst for righteousness.
24. *I am a builder of compassion in my family. "Finally, all of you, be like-minded, be sympathetic, love one another, be compassionate and humble." (1 Peter 3:8)*
    I declare that we are compassionate and humble, loving one another.
25. *I am a builder of perseverance in my family. "Blessed is the one who perseveres under trial because, having stood the test, that person will receive the crown of life that the Lord has promised to those who love him." (James 1:12)*
    I declare that we persevere under trial and receive the crown of life.
26. *I am a builder of faith in my family. "Now faith is confidence in what we hope for and*

assurance about what we do not see." (Hebrews 11:1)
I declare that we have confidence and assurance in our faith.

27. *I am a builder of service in my family. "For even the Son of Man came not to be served but to serve, and to give his life as a ransom for many." (Mark 10:45)*
    I declare that we serve one another in love.
28. *I am a builder of resilience in my family. "We are hard pressed on every side, but not crushed; perplexed, but not in despair; persecuted, but not abandoned; struck down, but not destroyed." (2 Corinthians 4:8-9)*
    I declare that we are resilient and not destroyed.
29. *I am a builder of truth in my family. "Sanctify them by the truth; your word is truth." (John 17:17)*
    I declare that we are sanctified by the truth of God's word.
30. *I am a builder of generosity in my family. "Give, and it will be given to you. A good measure, pressed down, shaken together and running over, will be poured into your lap. For with the measure you use, it will be measured to you." (Luke 6:38)*
    I declare that we give generously and receive abundantly.
31. *I am a builder of God's kingdom in my family. "But seek first his kingdom and his righteousness, and all these things will be given to you as well." (Matthew 6:33)*
    I declare that we seek first God's kingdom and righteousness.

Financial Abundance and Prosperity

1. *I am a builder of financial abundance. "The Lord will open the heavens, the storehouse of his bounty, to send rain on your land in season and to bless all the work of your hands." (Deuteronomy 28:12)*
   I declare that the Lord blesses all the work of my hands with abundance.
2. *I am a builder of prosperity. "Beloved, I pray that you may prosper in all things and be in health, just as your soul prospers." (3 John 1:2)*
   I declare that I prosper in all things and in health, just as my soul prospers.
3. *I am a builder of wealth. "The blessing of the Lord brings wealth, without painful toil for it." (Proverbs 10:22)*
   I declare that the blessing of the Lord brings me wealth without painful toil.
4. *I am a builder of generous giving. "Give, and it will be given to you. A good measure, pressed down, shaken together and running over, will be poured into your lap. For with the measure you use, it will be measured to you." (Luke 6:38)*
   I declare that I give generously, and it is given back to me in abundance.
5. *I am a builder of financial wisdom. "By wisdom a house is built, and through understanding it is established; through knowledge its rooms are filled with rare and beautiful treasures." (Proverbs 24:3-4)*
   I declare that I build my financial house with wisdom, understanding, and knowledge.

6. *I am a builder of savings. "Precious treasure and oil are in a wise man's dwelling, but a foolish man devours it." (Proverbs 21:20) I declare that I am wise and save precious treasures for the future.*
7. *I am a builder of investments. "Cast your bread upon the waters, for you will find it after many days." (Ecclesiastes 11:1) I declare that I invest wisely and reap the benefits in due time.*
8. *I am a builder of financial freedom. "The rich rule over the poor, and the borrower is slave to the lender." (Proverbs 22:7) I declare that I live in financial freedom, owing nothing but love.*
9. *I am a builder of generosity. "Each of you should give what you have decided in your heart to give, not reluctantly or under compulsion, for God loves a cheerful giver." (2 Corinthians 9:7) I declare that I am a cheerful giver, blessing others with my resources.*
10. *I am a builder of provision. "And my God will meet all your needs according to the riches of his glory in Christ Jesus." (Philippians 4:19) I declare that God meets all my needs according to His riches in glory.*
11. *I am a builder of financial peace. "Peace I leave with you; my peace I give to you. I do not give to you as the world gives. Do not let your hearts be troubled and do not be afraid." (John 14:27) I declare that I have financial peace and my heart is not troubled.*

12. I am a builder of faith in God's provision. "But seek first his kingdom and his righteousness, and all these things will be given to you as well." (Matthew 6:33)
I declare that I seek God's kingdom first, and all my financial needs are met.

13. I am a builder of contentment. "But godliness with contentment is great gain." (1 Timothy 6:6)
I declare that I am content and godly, which is great gain.

14. I am a builder of trust in God's plan. "For I know the plans I have for you, declares the Lord, plans for welfare and not for evil, to give you a future and a hope." (Jeremiah 29:11)
I declare that I trust in God's plan for my financial future.

15. I am a builder of financial stewardship. "Moreover, it is required of stewards that they be found trustworthy." (1 Corinthians 4:2)
I declare that I am a trustworthy steward of my finances.

16. I am a builder of financial growth. "I planted the seed, Apollos watered it, but God has been making it grow." (1 Corinthians 3:6)
I declare that God causes my financial growth.

17. I am a builder of financial abundance through hard work. "All hard work brings a profit, but mere talk leads only to poverty." (Proverbs 14:23)
I declare that my hard work brings profit and financial abundance.

18. I am a builder of financial blessings. "The Lord makes firm the steps of the one who delights in him." (Psalm 37:23)

I declare that the Lord makes firm my financial steps as I delight in Him.

19. *I am a builder of financial increase. "The Lord will grant you abundant prosperity—in the fruit of your womb, the young of your livestock and the crops of your ground—in the land he swore to your ancestors to give you." (Deuteronomy 28:11)*
    I declare that the Lord grants me abundant prosperity.
20. *I am a builder of financial harvest. "Let us not become weary in doing good, for at the proper time we will reap a harvest if we do not give up." (Galatians 6:9)*
    I declare that I will reap a financial harvest as I do good and do not give up.
21. *I am a builder of financial stability. "He is like a tree planted by streams of water that yields its fruit in its season, and its leaf does not wither. In all that he does, he prospers." (Psalm 1:3)*
    I declare that I am like a tree planted by streams of water, prospering in all I do.
22. *I am a builder of financial blessings for others. "You will be enriched in every way so that you can be generous on every occasion, and through us your generosity will result in thanksgiving to God." (2 Corinthians 9:11)*
    I declare that I am enriched to be generous, resulting in thanksgiving to God.
23. *I am a builder of financial abundance through obedience. "If you fully obey the Lord your God and carefully follow all his commands I give you today, the Lord your God will set you high above all the nations on earth." (Deuteronomy 28:1)*

I declare that my obedience to God brings financial abundance.

24. *I am a builder of financial freedom through God's power. "But remember the Lord your God, for it is he who gives you the ability to produce wealth, and so confirms his covenant, which he swore to your ancestors, as it is today." (Deuteronomy 8:18)*
    I declare that God gives me the ability to produce wealth.
25. *I am a builder of financial wisdom through God's word. "Your word is a lamp for my feet, a light on my path." (Psalm 119:105)*
    I declare that God's word guides my financial decisions.
26. *I am a builder of financial prosperity through God's favor. "Surely, Lord, you bless the righteous; you surround them with your favor as with a shield." (Psalm 5:12)*
    I declare that God's favor surrounds me and brings prosperity.
27. *I am a builder of financial success through diligence. "The plans of the diligent lead surely to abundance, but everyone who is hasty comes only to poverty." (Proverbs 21:5)*
    I declare that my diligent plans lead to abundance.
28. *I am a builder of financial stability through God's provision. "And God is able to bless you abundantly, so that in all things at all times, having all that you need, you will abound in every good work." (2 Corinthians 9:8)*
    I declare that God blesses me abundantly, so I have all I need to abound in good work.

29. *I am a builder of financial generosity through God's grace. "And God is able to make all grace abound to you, so that having all sufficiency in all things at all times, you may abound in every good work." (2 Corinthians 9:8)*
    I declare that God's grace makes all things sufficient for me.
30. *I am a builder of financial abundance through faith. "And whatever you ask in prayer, you will receive, if you have faith." (Matthew 21:22)*
    I declare that my faith brings financial abundance.
31. *I am a builder of financial success through God's promises. "For no matter how many promises God has made, they are 'Yes' in Christ. And so through him the 'Amen' is spoken by us to the glory of God." (2 Corinthians 1:20)*
    I declare that God's promises bring financial success.

Business

1. *I am a builder of successful ventures. "Commit to the Lord whatever you do, and he will establish your plans." (Proverbs 16:3)*
   I declare that my business ventures are committed to the Lord, and He establishes my plans.
2. *I am a builder of integrity in business. "The integrity of the upright guides them, but the unfaithful are destroyed by their duplicity." (Proverbs 11:3)*
   I declare that my business is guided by integrity.

3. *I am a builder of prosperity. "But remember the Lord your God, for it is he who gives you the ability to produce wealth." (Deuteronomy 8:18)*
   I declare that God gives me the ability to produce wealth through my business.
4. *I am a builder of ethical practices. "Better is a little with righteousness than great revenues with injustice." (Proverbs 16:8)*
   I declare that my business operates with righteousness and ethical practices.
5. *I am a builder of innovative solutions. "See, I am doing a new thing! Now it springs up; do you not perceive it?" (Isaiah 43:19)*
   I declare that I perceive and implement new and innovative solutions in my business.
6. *I am a builder of customer satisfaction. "Do to others as you would have them do to you." (Luke 6:31)*
   I declare that I treat my customers with the utmost respect and care.
7. *I am a builder of wise investments. "The plans of the diligent lead surely to abundance, but everyone who is hasty comes only to poverty." (Proverbs 21:5)*
   I declare that my diligent planning leads to abundant investments.
8. *I am a builder of a strong team. "Two are better than one, because they have a good return for their labor." (Ecclesiastes 4:9)*
   I declare that my team works together for a good return on our labor.
9. *I am a builder of excellence. "Whatever you do, work at it with all your heart, as working for the Lord, not for human masters." (Colossians*

3:23)
I declare that my business operates in excellence, working as unto the Lord.

10. *I am a builder of resilience. "For though the righteous fall seven times, they rise again." (Proverbs 24:16)*
    I declare that my business rises again, no matter how many times it falls.
11. *I am a builder of faith-driven success. "Have faith in God," Jesus answered. "Truly I tell you, if anyone says to this mountain, 'Go, throw yourself into the sea,' and does not doubt in their heart but believes that what they say will happen, it will be done for them." (Mark 11:22-23)*
    I declare that my business success is driven by faith in God.
12. *I am a builder of financial wisdom. "For where your treasure is, there your heart will be also." (Matthew 6:21)*
    I declare that my heart is aligned with God's wisdom in financial matters.
13. *I am a builder of strong foundations. "Therefore everyone who hears these words of mine and puts them into practice is like a wise man who built his house on the rock." (Matthew 7:24)*
    I declare that my business is built on strong, unshakable foundations.
14. *I am a builder of strategic alliances. "Plans fail for lack of counsel, but with many advisers they succeed." (Proverbs 15:22)*
    I declare that my business plans succeed with the counsel of many advisers.

15. I am a builder of community impact. "You are the light of the world. A town built on a hill cannot be hidden." (Matthew 5:14)
I declare that my business is a light to the community, impacting it positively.

16. I am a builder of growth. "So neither the one who plants nor the one who waters is anything, but only God, who makes things grow." (1 Corinthians 3:7)
I declare that God causes my business to grow.

17. I am a builder of lasting legacy. "A good person leaves an inheritance for their children's children." (Proverbs 13:22)
I declare that my business leaves a lasting legacy for future generations.

18. I am a builder of opportunities. "I can do all this through him who gives me strength." (Philippians 4:13)
I declare that through Christ, I create opportunities and overcome challenges.

19. I am a builder of trust and loyalty. "Whoever walks in integrity walks securely." (Proverbs 10:9)
I declare that my integrity builds trust and loyalty in my business.

20. I am a builder of strategic growth. "The plans of the diligent lead surely to abundance." (Proverbs 21:5)
I declare that my strategic planning leads to the abundant growth of my business.

21. I am a builder of God's kingdom through business. "But seek first his kingdom and his righteousness, and all these things will be given to you as well." (Matthew 6:33)

I declare that I seek God's kingdom first in my business endeavors.

22. *I am a builder of courage and boldness. "Have I not commanded you? Be strong and courageous. Do not be afraid; do not be discouraged, for the Lord your God will be with you wherever you go." (Joshua 1:9)*
    I declare that I am strong and courageous in my business decisions.
23. *I am a builder of strategic marketing. "Be wise as serpents and innocent as doves." (Matthew 10:16)*
    I declare that my marketing strategies are wise and effective.
24. *I am a builder of efficient processes. "Let all things be done decently and in order." (1 Corinthians 14:40)*
    I declare that my business processes are efficient and orderly.
25. *I am a builder of global impact. "Go into all the world and preach the gospel to all creation." (Mark 16:15)*
    I declare that my business reaches and impacts the global market.
26. *I am a builder of God's provision. "And my God will meet all your needs according to the riches of his glory in Christ Jesus." (Philippians 4:19)*
    I declare that God meets all my business needs.
27. *I am a builder of faith-driven ventures. "Now faith is confidence in what we hope for and assurance about what we do not see." (Hebrews 11:1)*

I declare that my business ventures are driven by faith.

28. *I am a builder of divine partnerships. "Iron sharpens iron, and one man sharpens another." (Proverbs 27:17)*
    I declare that I form divine partnerships that sharpen and enhance my business.
29. *I am a builder of God's wisdom in business. "For the Lord gives wisdom; from his mouth come knowledge and understanding." (Proverbs 2:6)*
    I declare that I operate my business with God's wisdom, knowledge, and understanding.
30. *I am a builder of abundant harvests. "Those who sow with tears will reap with songs of joy." (Psalm 126:5)*
    I declare that I reap abundant harvests from my business efforts.
31. *I am a builder of God's purpose in business. "Many are the plans in a person's heart, but it is the Lord's purpose that prevails." (Proverbs 19:21)*
    I declare that my business aligns with God's purpose, which prevails.

Market Dominance

1. *I am a builder of market leadership. "The Lord will make you the head, not the tail. If you pay attention to the commands of the Lord your God that I give you this day and carefully follow them, you will always be at the top, never at the bottom." (Deuteronomy 28:13)*
   I declare that I am the head and not the tail in the market.

2. *I am a builder of strategic influence. "You are the light of the world. A town built on a hill cannot be hidden." (Matthew 5:14)*
   I declare that my business shines as a light in the marketplace.
3. *I am a builder of innovative leadership. "Behold, I am doing a new thing; now it springs forth, do you not perceive it?" (Isaiah 43:19)*
   I declare that I lead with innovation and foresight.
4. *I am a builder of competitive advantage. "Do not be conformed to this world, but be transformed by the renewal of your mind." (Romans 12:2)*
   I declare that my renewed mind gives me a competitive edge.
5. *I am a builder of market influence. "The righteous will never be shaken; they will be remembered forever." (Psalm 112:6)*
   I declare that my influence in the market will be remembered forever.
6. *I am a builder of strong brand presence. "A good name is more desirable than great riches; to be esteemed is better than silver or gold." (Proverbs 22:1)*
   I declare that my brand name is esteemed and highly regarded.
7. *I am a builder of market trust. "Whoever walks in integrity walks securely." (Proverbs 10:9)*
   I declare that my integrity builds trust in the marketplace.
8. *I am a builder of market innovation. "By wisdom a house is built, and through understanding it is established." (Proverbs*

24:3)
I declare that my wisdom and understanding drive market innovation.

9. *I am a builder of market resilience. "The Lord is my rock, my fortress, and my deliverer; my God is my rock, in whom I take refuge." (Psalm 18:2)*
   I declare that my business is resilient and unshakable.
10. *I am a builder of industry leadership. "The plans of the diligent lead surely to abundance." (Proverbs 21:5)*
    I declare that my diligent plans lead to industry leadership.
11. *I am a builder of lasting impact. "I can do all this through him who gives me strength." (Philippians 4:13)*
    I declare that I make a lasting impact in the market through Christ's strength.
12. *I am a builder of customer loyalty. "Do to others as you would have them do to you." (Luke 6:31)*
    I declare that I build customer loyalty by treating them as I want to be treated.
13. *I am a builder of strategic marketing. "Be wise as serpents and innocent as doves." (Matthew 10:16)*
    I declare that my marketing strategies are wise and effective.
14. *I am a builder of market expansion. "Enlarge the place of your tent, stretch your tent curtains wide, do not hold back; lengthen your cords, strengthen your stakes." (Isaiah 54:2)*
    I declare that I expand and strengthen my market presence.

15. *I am a builder of divine strategies. "Commit to the Lord whatever you do, and he will establish your plans." (Proverbs 16:3)*
    I declare that my market strategies are established by the Lord.
16. *I am a builder of visionary leadership. "Where there is no vision, the people perish." (Proverbs 29:18)*
    I declare that my visionary leadership guides my market success.
17. *I am a builder of market excellence. "Whatever you do, work at it with all your heart, as working for the Lord." (Colossians 3:23)*
    I declare that my business operates with excellence.
18. *I am a builder of market influence. "You will be for me a kingdom of priests and a holy nation." (Exodus 19:6)*
    I declare that I influence the market with my kingdom mindset.
19. *I am a builder of strategic growth. "The plans of the diligent lead surely to abundance." (Proverbs 21:5)*
    I declare that my diligent planning leads to strategic market growth.
20. *I am a builder of ethical dominance. "Better is a little with righteousness than great revenues with injustice." (Proverbs 16:8)*
    I declare that my market dominance is built on righteousness.
21. *I am a builder of resilience in market challenges. "For though the righteous fall seven times, they rise again." (Proverbs 24:16)*

I declare that I rise again, no matter the market challenges.

22. *I am a builder of global market presence. "Go into all the world and preach the gospel to all creation." (Mark 16:15)*
    I declare that my business impacts the global market.
23. *I am a builder of market solutions. "I am doing a new thing! Now it springs up; do you not perceive it?" (Isaiah 43:19)*
    I declare that I perceive and implement market solutions.
24. *I am a builder of divine influence. "You are the salt of the earth." (Matthew 5:13)*
    I declare that my influence in the market is like salt, adding value and flavor.
25. *I am a builder of strategic partnerships. "Iron sharpens iron, and one man sharpens another." (Proverbs 27:17)*
    I declare that I form strategic partnerships that sharpen my market strategies.
26. *I am a builder of market opportunities. "I can do all this through him who gives me strength." (Philippians 4:13)*
    I declare that I create market opportunities through Christ's strength.
27. *I am a builder of market innovation. "Behold, I am doing a new thing; now it springs forth, do you not perceive it?" (Isaiah 43:19)*
    I declare that I lead with innovation in the market.
28. *I am a builder of ethical market practices. "The integrity of the upright guides them." (Proverbs 11:3)*

I declare that my market practices are guided by integrity.

29. *I am a builder of market trust. "Whoever walks in integrity walks securely." (Proverbs 10:9) I declare that my integrity builds trust in the marketplace.*
30. *I am a builder of divine strategies. "Commit to the Lord whatever you do, and he will establish your plans." (Proverbs 16:3) I declare that my market strategies are established by the Lord.*
31. *I am a builder of God's kingdom in the market. "But seek first his kingdom and his righteousness, and all these things will be given to you as well." (Matthew 6:33) I declare that I seek God's kingdom first in my market endeavors.*

Leadership and Influence

1. *I am a builder of godly leadership. "For the Lord gives wisdom; from his mouth come knowledge and understanding." (Proverbs 2:6) I declare that my leadership is built on God's wisdom and understanding.*
2. *I am a builder of servant leadership. "But among you it will be different. Whoever wants to be a leader among you must be your servant." (Matthew 20:26) I declare that I lead by serving others.*
3. *I am a builder of influential leadership. "You are the light of the world. A town built on a hill cannot be hidden." (Matthew 5:14) I declare that my leadership shines as a light to others.*

4. *I am a builder of visionary leadership. "Where there is no vision, the people perish." (Proverbs 29:18)*
   I declare that my vision guides my leadership.
5. *I am a builder of courageous leadership. "Have I not commanded you? Be strong and courageous. Do not be afraid; do not be discouraged, for the Lord your God will be with you wherever you go." (Joshua 1:9)*
   I declare that I lead with strength and courage.
6. *I am a builder of compassionate leadership. "Be kind and compassionate to one another." (Ephesians 4:32)*
   I declare that my leadership is marked by kindness and compassion.
7. *I am a builder of righteous leadership. "Righteousness exalts a nation, but sin condemns any people." (Proverbs 14:34)*
   I declare that my leadership exalts through righteousness.
8. *I am a builder of wise leadership. "The fear of the Lord is the beginning of wisdom, and knowledge of the Holy One is understanding." (Proverbs 9:10)*
   I declare that my leadership is grounded in the wisdom and knowledge of the Lord.
9. *I am a builder of enduring influence. "I can do all this through him who gives me strength." (Philippians 4:13)*
   I declare that my influence endures through Christ's strength.
10. *I am a builder of humble leadership. "Do nothing out of selfish ambition or vain conceit. Rather, in humility value others above yourselves." (Philippians 2:3)*

I declare that my leadership values others in humility.

11. *I am a builder of integrity in leadership. "The integrity of the upright guides them." (Proverbs 11:3)*
    I declare that my leadership is guided by integrity.
12. *I am a builder of inspiring leadership. "Therefore encourage one another and build each other up." (1 Thessalonians 5:11)*
    I declare that my leadership encourages and builds others up.
13. *I am a builder of peace in leadership. "Blessed are the peacemakers, for they will be called children of God." (Matthew 5:9)*
    I declare that my leadership fosters peace.
14. *I am a builder of strategic influence. "Plans fail for lack of counsel, but with many advisers they succeed." (Proverbs 15:22)*
    I declare that my leadership succeeds with strategic counsel.
15. *I am a builder of faith-driven leadership. "Have faith in God," Jesus answered. "Truly I tell you, if anyone says to this mountain, 'Go, throw yourself into the sea,' and does not doubt in their heart but believes that what they say will happen, it will be done for them." (Mark 11:22-23)*
    I declare that my leadership is driven by faith in God.
16. *I am a builder of love in leadership. "Above all, love each other deeply, because love covers over a multitude of sins." (1 Peter 4:8)*
    I declare that my leadership is rooted in love.

17. I am a builder of disciplined leadership. "For the Spirit God gave us does not make us timid, but gives us power, love and self-discipline." (2 Timothy 1:7)
I declare that my leadership is marked by power, love, and self-discipline.

18. I am a builder of strategic vision. "Write down the revelation and make it plain on tablets so that a herald may run with it." (Habakkuk 2:2)
I declare that my vision is clear and strategic.

19. I am a builder of transformative influence. "Do not conform to the pattern of this world, but be transformed by the renewing of your mind." (Romans 12:2)
I declare that my influence transforms through a renewed mind.

20. I am a builder of resilient leadership. "For though the righteous fall seven times, they rise again." (Proverbs 24:16)
I declare that my leadership is resilient and rises again.

21. I am a builder of inclusive leadership. "There is neither Jew nor Gentile, neither slave nor free, nor is there male and female, for you are all one in Christ Jesus." (Galatians 3:28)
I declare that my leadership is inclusive and unifying.

22. I am a builder of impactful leadership. "I can do all this through him who gives me strength." (Philippians 4:13)
I declare that my leadership impacts others through Christ's strength.

23. I am a builder of ethical influence. "Better is a little with righteousness than great revenues with injustice." (Proverbs 16:8)

I declare that my influence is built on righteousness.

24. *I am a builder of community in leadership. "Let us consider how we may spur one another on toward love and good deeds." (Hebrews 10:24)*
    I declare that my leadership builds community and encourages good deeds.
25. *I am a builder of strategic alliances. "Two are better than one, because they have a good return for their labor." (Ecclesiastes 4:9)*
    I declare that my leadership forms strategic alliances for greater impact.
26. *I am a builder of empowering leadership. "I can do all this through him who gives me strength." (Philippians 4:13)*
    I declare that my leadership empowers others through Christ's strength.
27. *I am a builder of ethical leadership. "The integrity of the upright guides them." (Proverbs 11:3)*
    I declare that my leadership is guided by integrity.
28. *I am a builder of wise influence. "The fear of the Lord is the beginning of wisdom, and knowledge of the Holy One is understanding." (Proverbs 9:10)*
    I declare that my influence is grounded in the wisdom and knowledge of the Lord.
29. *I am a builder of strategic influence. "Plans fail for lack of counsel, but with many advisers they succeed." (Proverbs 15:22)*
    I declare that my influence succeeds with strategic counsel.

30. *I am a builder of servant influence. "But among you it will be different. Whoever wants to be a leader among you must be your servant." (Matthew 20:26)*
I declare that my influence serves others.
31. *I am a builder of God's kingdom through leadership. "But seek first his kingdom and his righteousness, and all these things will be given to you as well." (Matthew 6:33)*
I declare that my leadership seeks God's kingdom first.

Projects for Community and Well being of Society

1. *I am a builder of hope in my community, believing that with God, all things are possible. "With man this is impossible, but with God all things are possible." (Matthew 19:26)*
2. *I am a builder of unity, striving to maintain the bond of peace through the Holy Spirit. "Make every effort to keep the unity of the Spirit through the bond of peace." (Ephesians 4:3)*
3. *I am a builder of love, letting my actions be a reflection of God's unconditional love. "Do everything in love." (1 Corinthians 16:14)*
4. *I am a builder of justice, acting fairly and seeking righteousness in all my endeavors. "He has shown you, O mortal, what is good. And what does the Lord require of you? To act justly and to love mercy and to walk humbly with your God." (Micah 6:8)*
5. *I am a builder of compassion, showing mercy to those in need, as Jesus taught. "Be merciful, just as your Father is merciful." (Luke 6:36)*

6. *I am a builder of faith, strengthening the hearts of those around me. "And let us consider how we may spur one another on toward love and good deeds." (Hebrews 10:24)*
7. *I am a builder of wisdom, using the knowledge God gives to benefit my community. "If any of you lacks wisdom, you should ask God, who gives generously to all without finding fault, and it will be given to you." (James 1:5)*
8. *I am a builder of peace, fostering harmony and understanding in all relationships. "Blessed are the peacemakers, for they will be called children of God." (Matthew 5:9)*
9. *I am a builder of strength, empowering others through the joy of the Lord. "Do not grieve, for the joy of the Lord is your strength." (Nehemiah 8:10)*
10. *I am a builder of resilience, helping my community to stand firm in times of trial. "Blessed is the one who perseveres under trial because, having stood the test, that person will receive the crown of life that the Lord has promised to those who love him." (James 1:12)*
11. *I am a builder of prosperity, believing that God will supply all our needs. "And my God will meet all your needs according to the riches of his glory in Christ Jesus." (Philippians 4:19)*
12. *I am a builder of kindness, doing unto others as I would have them do unto me. "So in everything, do to others what you would have them do to you, for this sums up the Law and the Prophets." (Matthew 7:12)*

13. *I am a builder of light, shining brightly in a world that needs God's truth. "You are the light of the world. A town built on a hill cannot be hidden." (Matthew 5:14)*
14. *I am a builder of healing, offering support and encouragement to the broken-hearted. "He heals the brokenhearted and binds up their wounds." (Psalm 147:3)*
15. *I am a builder of generosity, giving freely as I have received from God. "Each of you should give what you have decided in your heart to give, not reluctantly or under compulsion, for God loves a cheerful giver." (2 Corinthians 9:7)*
16. *I am a builder of joy, spreading the good news of Jesus Christ. "May the God of hope fill you with all joy and peace as you trust in him, so that you may overflow with hope by the power of the Holy Spirit." (Romans 15:13)*
17. *I am a builder of patience, enduring trials with faith and hope. "Be joyful in hope, patient in affliction, faithful in prayer." (Romans 12:12)*
18. *I am a builder of innovation, using my God-given creativity to solve problems. "I, wisdom, dwell together with prudence; I possess knowledge and discretion." (Proverbs 8:12)*
19. *I am a builder of integrity, living a life that honors God in all I do. "Whoever walks in integrity walks securely, but whoever takes crooked paths will be found out." (Proverbs 10:9)*
20. *I am a builder of education, valuing wisdom and understanding. "The beginning of wisdom is this: Get wisdom. Though it cost all you have, get understanding." (Proverbs 4:7)*

21. *I am a builder of joy, delighting in the work God has given me. "Take delight in the Lord, and he will give you the desires of your heart." (Psalm 37:4)*
22. *I am a builder of trust, fostering relationships built on God's truth. "It is better to take refuge in the Lord than to trust in humans." (Psalm 118:8)*
23. *I am a builder of service, following Jesus' example of servant leadership. "For even the Son of Man did not come to be served, but to serve, and to give his life as a ransom for many." (Mark 10:45)*
24. *I am a builder of creativity, using my talents for the glory of God. "Whatever you do, work at it with all your heart, as working for the Lord, not for human masters." (Colossians 3:23)*
25. *I am a builder of courage, standing firm in my convictions. "Have I not commanded you? Be strong and courageous. Do not be afraid; do not be discouraged, for the Lord your God will be with you wherever you go." (Joshua 1:9)*
26. *I am a builder of fellowship, encouraging one another in love. "Not giving up meeting together, as some are in the habit of doing, but encouraging one another—and all the more as you see the Day approaching." (Hebrews 10:25)*
27. *I am a builder of endurance, running the race with perseverance. "Therefore, since we are surrounded by such a great cloud of witnesses, let us throw off everything that hinders and the sin that so easily entangles. And let us run with perseverance the race marked out for us." (Hebrews 12:1)*

28. *I am a builder of compassion, seeing others through the eyes of Christ. "Therefore, as God's chosen people, holy and dearly loved, clothe yourselves with compassion, kindness, humility, gentleness and patience." (Colossians 3:12)*
29. *I am a builder of honor, respecting and valuing each person. "Show proper respect to everyone, love the family of believers, fear God, honor the emperor." (1 Peter 2:17)*
30. *I am a builder of prayer, lifting my community up to the Lord. "Pray continually." (1 Thessalonians 5:17)*
31. *I am a builder of blessings, speaking life and God's promises over my community. "The Lord bless you and keep you; the Lord make his face shine on you and be gracious to you; the Lord turn his face toward you and give you peace." (Numbers 6:24-26)*

Relationships and Communication

1. *I am a builder of strong relationships. "Two are better than one, because they have a good return for their labor: If either of them falls down, one can help the other up." (Ecclesiastes 4:9-10)*
   I declare that I build strong relationships that provide support and partnership.
2. *I am a builder of effective communication. "Let your conversation be always full of grace, seasoned with salt, so that you may know how to answer everyone." (Colossians 4:6)*
   I declare that my communication is full of grace and wisdom.

3. *I am a builder of love in my relationships. "Above all, love each other deeply, because love covers over a multitude of sins." (1 Peter 4:8)*
   I declare that I love deeply, and it covers a multitude of sins.
4. *I am a builder of trust in my relationships. "Whoever walks in integrity walks securely, but whoever takes crooked paths will be found out." (Proverbs 10:9)*
   I declare that I walk in integrity, building trust in my relationships.
5. *I am a builder of empathy in my communication. "Rejoice with those who rejoice; mourn with those who mourn." (Romans 12:15)*
   I declare that I empathize with others, sharing in their joys and sorrows.
6. *I am a builder of patience in my relationships. "Be completely humble and gentle; be patient, bearing with one another in love." (Ephesians 4:2)*
   I declare that I bear with others in love, building patience in my relationships.
7. *I am a builder of peace through my words. "Blessed are the peacemakers, for they will be called children of God." (Matthew 5:9)*
   I declare that I speak words that make peace.
8. *I am a builder of joy in my interactions. "A cheerful heart is good medicine, but a crushed spirit dries up the bones." (Proverbs 17:22)*
   I declare that my interactions bring joy and cheer to others.
9. *I am a builder of wisdom in my communication. "The one who has knowledge*

uses words with restraint, and whoever has understanding is even-tempered." (Proverbs 17:27)
I declare that I use my words with restraint and understanding.

10. *I am a builder of understanding in my relationships. "The purposes of a person's heart are deep waters, but one who has insight draws them out." (Proverbs 20:5)*
    I declare that I draw out understanding and insight in my relationships.
11. *I am a builder of forgiveness in my relationships. "Be kind and compassionate to one another, forgiving each other, just as in Christ God forgave you." (Ephesians 4:32)*
    I declare that I forgive others as Christ forgave me.
12. *I am a builder of unity in my communication. "How good and pleasant it is when God's people live together in unity!" (Psalm 133:1)*
    I declare that my communication fosters unity.
13. *I am a builder of encouragement through my words. "Therefore encourage one another and build each other up, just as in fact you are doing." (1 Thessalonians 5:11)*
    I declare that I encourage and build others up with my words.
14. *I am a builder of respect in my relationships. "Show proper respect to everyone, love the family of believers, fear God, honor the emperor." (1 Peter 2:17)*
    I declare that I show proper respect to everyone.
15. *I am a builder of kindness in my communication. "Be kind and compassionate*

to one another, forgiving each other, just as in Christ God forgave you." (Ephesians 4:32)
I declare that my words are kind and compassionate.

16. *I am a builder of truth in my relationships. "Therefore each of you must put off falsehood and speak truthfully to your neighbor, for we are all members of one body." (Ephesians 4:25)*
    I declare that I speak truthfully in my relationships.
17. *I am a builder of listening in my communication. "My dear brothers and sisters, take note of this: Everyone should be quick to listen, slow to speak and slow to become angry." (James 1:19)*
    I declare that I am quick to listen and slow to speak.
18. *I am a builder of reconciliation in my relationships. "If it is possible, as far as it depends on you, live at peace with everyone." (Romans 12:18)*
    I declare that I seek reconciliation and peace in my relationships.
19. *I am a builder of gratitude in my communication. "Give thanks in all circumstances; for this is God's will for you in Christ Jesus." (1 Thessalonians 5:18)*
    I declare that I express gratitude in all my communication.
20. *I am a builder of humility in my relationships. "Do nothing out of selfish ambition or vain conceit. Rather, in humility value others above yourselves." (Philippians 2:3)*

I declare that I value others above myself in humility.

21. *I am a builder of wisdom in my communication. "The one who has knowledge uses words with restraint, and whoever has understanding is even-tempered." (Proverbs 17:27)*
    I declare that I use words with restraint and understanding.
22. *I am a builder of trust in my relationships. "Whoever walks in integrity walks securely, but whoever takes crooked paths will be found out." (Proverbs 10:9)*
    I declare that I walk in integrity, building trust in my relationships.
23. *I am a builder of love in my relationships. "Above all, love each other deeply, because love covers over a multitude of sins." (1 Peter 4:8)*
    I declare that I love deeply, and it covers a multitude of sins.
24. *I am a builder of patience in my communication. "Be completely humble and gentle; be patient, bearing with one another in love." (Ephesians 4:2)*
    I declare that I bear with others in love, building patience in my communication.
25. *I am a builder of peace through my words. "Blessed are the peacemakers, for they will be called children of God." (Matthew 5:9)*
    I declare that I speak words that make peace.
26. *I am a builder of joy in my relationships. "A cheerful heart is good medicine, but a crushed spirit dries up the bones." (Proverbs 17:22)*

I declare that my relationships bring joy and cheer to others.

27. *I am a builder of empathy in my communication. "Rejoice with those who rejoice; mourn with those who mourn." (Romans 12:15)*
    I declare that I empathize with others, sharing in their joys and sorrows.
28. *I am a builder of encouragement through my words. "Therefore encourage one another and build each other up, just as in fact you are doing." (1 Thessalonians 5:11)*
    I declare that I encourage and build others up with my words.
29. *I am a builder of truth in my relationships. "Therefore each of you must put off falsehood and speak truthfully to your neighbor, for we are all members of one body." (Ephesians 4:25)*
    I declare that I speak truthfully in my relationships.
30. *I am a builder of kindness in my communication. "Be kind and compassionate to one another, forgiving each other, just as in Christ God forgave you." (Ephesians 4:32)*
    I declare that my words are kind and compassionate.
31. *I am a builder of reconciliation in my relationships. "If it is possible, as far as it depends on you, live at peace with everyone." (Romans 12:18)*
    I declare that I seek reconciliation and peace in my relationships.

Patience and Resilience

1. *I am a builder of patience in my spirit. "But if we hope for what we do not see, we wait for it with patience." (Romans 8:25)*
   I declare that I wait patiently for God's promises.
2. *I am a builder of resilience through trials. "Consider it pure joy, my brothers and sisters, whenever you face trials of many kinds, because you know that the testing of your faith produces perseverance." (James 1:2-3)*
   I declare that my faith is strengthened through trials.
3. *I am a builder of steadfast patience. "Be still before the Lord and wait patiently for him." (Psalm 37:7)*
   I declare that I am still and wait for the Lord.
4. *I am a builder of enduring resilience. "But those who hope in the Lord will renew their strength. They will soar on wings like eagles; they will run and not grow weary, they will walk and not be faint." (Isaiah 40:31)*
   I declare that my hope in the Lord renews my strength.
5. *I am a builder of patience in adversity. "The end of a matter is better than its beginning, and patience is better than pride." (Ecclesiastes 7:8)*
   I declare that my patience endures through adversity.
6. *I am a builder of resilient faith. "I can do all this through him who gives me strength." (Philippians 4:13)*
   I declare that my resilience comes from Christ's strength.

7. *I am a builder of patient endurance. "You need to persevere so that when you have done the will of God, you will receive what he has promised." (Hebrews 10:36)*
   I declare that I persevere to receive God's promises.
8. *I am a builder of resilience in the Lord. "The Lord is my rock, my fortress and my deliverer; my God is my rock, in whom I take refuge." (Psalm 18:2)*
   I declare that my resilience is founded in the Lord.
9. *I am a builder of patient wisdom. "A hot-tempered person stirs up conflict, but the one who is patient calms a quarrel." (Proverbs 15:18)*
   I declare that my patience brings peace and wisdom.
10. *I am a builder of resilient hope. "We rejoice in our sufferings, knowing that suffering produces endurance." (Romans 5:3)*
    I declare that my hope is resilient in suffering.
11. *I am a builder of patience in waiting. "The Lord is good to those whose hope is in him, to the one who seeks him." (Lamentations 3:25)*
    I declare that my patience is rewarded by the Lord's goodness.
12. *I am a builder of resilient joy. "The joy of the Lord is your strength." (Nehemiah 8:10)*
    I declare that my joy in the Lord gives me resilience.
13. *I am a builder of patient love. "Love is patient, love is kind." (1 Corinthians 13:4)*
    I declare that my love is patient and kind.

14. *I am a builder of resilience in faith. "For we live by faith, not by sight." (2 Corinthians 5:7) I declare that my resilience is strengthened by faith.*
15. *I am a builder of patient perseverance. "Let us not become weary in doing good, for at the proper time we will reap a harvest if we do not give up." (Galatians 6:9) I declare that I persevere in doing good.*
16. *I am a builder of resilient character. "Not only so, but we also glory in our sufferings, because we know that suffering produces perseverance; perseverance, character; and character, hope." (Romans 5:3-4) I declare that my character is resilient through perseverance.*
17. *I am a builder of patient strength. "The Lord is my strength and my shield; my heart trusts in him, and he helps me." (Psalm 28:7) I declare that my strength is built through patience.*
18. *I am a builder of resilient faithfulness. "Let us hold unswervingly to the hope we profess, for he who promised is faithful." (Hebrews 10:23) I declare that my faithfulness is resilient.*
19. *I am a builder of patient humility. "Be completely humble and gentle; be patient, bearing with one another in love." (Ephesians 4:2) I declare that my humility is built through patience.*
20. *I am a builder of resilient joy in the Lord. "Rejoice in the Lord always. I will say it again: Rejoice!" (Philippians 4:4) I declare that my joy in the Lord is resilient.*

21. *I am a builder of patient hope. "But if we hope for what we do not yet have, we wait for it patiently." (Romans 8:25)*
    I declare that my hope is patient.
22. *I am a builder of resilient perseverance. "Let perseverance finish its work so that you may be mature and complete, not lacking anything." (James 1:4)*
    I declare that my perseverance builds resilience.
23. *I am a builder of patient understanding. "Whoever is patient has great understanding, but one who is quick-tempered displays folly." (Proverbs 14:29)*
    I declare that my patience brings understanding.
24. *I am a builder of resilient spirit. "For the Spirit God gave us does not make us timid, but gives us power, love and self-discipline." (2 Timothy 1:7)*
    I declare that my spirit is resilient through God's power.
25. *I am a builder of patient endurance. "Blessed is the one who perseveres under trial because, having stood the test, that person will receive the crown of life that the Lord has promised to those who love him." (James 1:12)*
    I declare that I endure trials with patience.
26. *I am a builder of resilient hope. "But those who hope in the Lord will renew their strength." (Isaiah 40:31)*
    I declare that my hope in the Lord renews my strength.

27. *I am a builder of patient love. "Love is patient, love is kind." (1 Corinthians 13:4)*
    I declare that my love is patient and kind.
28. *I am a builder of resilient faith. "For we live by faith, not by sight." (2 Corinthians 5:7)*
    I declare that my faith is resilient.
29. *I am a builder of patient perseverance. "Let us not become weary in doing good, for at the proper time we will reap a harvest if we do not give up." (Galatians 6:9)*
    I declare that I persevere in doing good.
30. *I am a builder of resilient character. "Not only so, but we also glory in our sufferings, because we know that suffering produces perseverance; perseverance, character; and character, hope." (Romans 5:3-4)*
    I declare that my character is resilient through perseverance.
31. *I am a builder of patient strength. "The Lord is my strength and my shield; my heart trusts in him, and he helps me." (Psalm 28:7)*
    I declare that my strength is built through patience.

Empathy and Compassion

1. *I am a builder of compassionate love. "Be kind and compassionate to one another, forgiving each other, just as in Christ God forgave you." (Ephesians 4:32)*
   I declare that my compassion reflects God's forgiveness.
2. *I am a builder of empathetic understanding. "Rejoice with those who rejoice; mourn with those who mourn." (Romans 12:15)*

I declare that I empathize with others' joys and sorrows.

3. *I am a builder of heartfelt compassion. "Finally, all of you, be like-minded, be sympathetic, love one another, be compassionate and humble." (1 Peter 3:8)*
   I declare that my heart is filled with compassion and humility.
4. *I am a builder of Christ-like empathy. "Carry each other's burdens, and in this way you will fulfill the law of Christ." (Galatians 6:2)*
   I declare that I carry others' burdens with empathy.
5. *I am a builder of merciful compassion. "Blessed are the merciful, for they will be shown mercy." (Matthew 5:7)*
   I declare that my compassion brings mercy.
6. *I am a builder of empathetic kindness. "Therefore, as God's chosen people, holy and dearly loved, clothe yourselves with compassion, kindness, humility, gentleness and patience." (Colossians 3:12)*
   I declare that I am clothed with compassion and kindness.
7. *I am a builder of godly empathy. "Finally, all of you, be like-minded, be sympathetic, love one another, be compassionate and humble." (1 Peter 3:8)*
   I declare that my empathy is godly and humble.
8. *I am a builder of compassionate service. "Each of you should use whatever gift you have received to serve others, as faithful stewards of God's grace in its various forms." (1 Peter 4:10)*

I declare that my service is marked by compassion.

9. *I am a builder of empathetic love. "Love each other with genuine affection, and take delight in honoring each other." (Romans 12:10)*
   I declare that my love is genuine and empathetic.
10. *I am a builder of compassion in action. "Dear children, let us not love with words or speech but with actions and in truth." (1 John 3:18)*
    I declare that my compassion is shown through actions.
11. *I am a builder of empathetic care. "Cast all your anxiety on him because he cares for you." (1 Peter 5:7)*
    I declare that my care for others reflects God's care for me.
12. *I am a builder of compassionate hearts. "Finally, all of you, be like-minded, be sympathetic, love one another, be compassionate and humble." (1 Peter 3:8)*
    I declare that my heart is filled with compassion.
13. *I am a builder of empathetic support. "Encourage one another and build each other up." (1 Thessalonians 5:11)*
    I declare that I support others with empathy.
14. *I am a builder of compassionate peace. "Make every effort to keep the unity of the Spirit through the bond of peace." (Ephesians 4:3)*
    I declare that my compassion brings peace.
15. *I am a builder of empathetic listening. "My dear brothers and sisters, take note of this: Everyone should be quick to listen, slow to speak and slow to become angry." (James*

1:19)
I declare that I listen with empathy.

16. *I am a builder of compassionate grace. "Let your conversation be always full of grace, seasoned with salt, so that you may know how to answer everyone." (Colossians 4:6)*
I declare that my words are full of compassionate grace.
17. *I am a builder of empathetic presence. "The Lord is close to the brokenhearted and saves those who are crushed in spirit." (Psalm 34:18)*
I declare that I am present with those who are hurting.
18. *I am a builder of compassionate action. "Do not merely listen to the word, and so deceive yourselves. Do what it says." (James 1:22)*
I declare that my compassion is shown through my actions.
19. *I am a builder of empathetic fellowship. "If one part suffers, every part suffers with it; if one part is honored, every part rejoices with it." (1 Corinthians 12:26)*
I declare that I share in others' sufferings and joys.
20. *I am a builder of compassionate love. "Be kind and compassionate to one another, forgiving each other, just as in Christ God forgave you." (Ephesians 4:32)*
I declare that my love is compassionate and forgiving.
21. *I am a builder of empathetic patience. "Be completely humble and gentle; be patient, bearing with one another in love." (Ephesians 4:2)*

I declare that my patience is empathetic and loving.

22. *I am a builder of compassionate humility. "Do nothing out of selfish ambition or vain conceit. Rather, in humility value others above yourselves." (Philippians 2:3)*
    I declare that my humility is compassionate.
23. *I am a builder of empathetic encouragement. "Therefore encourage one another and build each other up, just as in fact you are doing." (1 Thessalonians 5:11)*
    I declare that my encouragement is empathetic.
24. *I am a builder of compassionate community. "How good and pleasant it is when God's people live together in unity!" (Psalm 133:1)*
    I declare that my compassion fosters community.
25. *I am a builder of empathetic love. "Above all, love each other deeply, because love covers over a multitude of sins." (1 Peter 4:8)*
    I declare that my love is deep and empathetic.
26. *I am a builder of compassionate strength. "The Lord is my strength and my shield; my heart trusts in him, and he helps me." (Psalm 28:7)*
    I declare that my strength is built on compassion.
27. *I am a builder of empathetic generosity. "Each of you should give what you have decided in your heart to give, not reluctantly or under compulsion, for God loves a cheerful giver." (2 Corinthians 9:7)*
    I declare that my generosity is empathetic.

28. *I am a builder of compassionate unity. "Make every effort to keep the unity of the Spirit through the bond of peace." (Ephesians 4:3) I declare that my compassion fosters unity.*
29. *I am a builder of empathetic peace. "Blessed are the peacemakers, for they will be called children of God." (Matthew 5:9) I declare that my empathy makes peace.*
30. *I am a builder of compassionate service. "Serve one another humbly in love." (Galatians 5:13) I declare that my service is humble and compassionate.*
31. *I am a builder of empathetic faith. "Be completely humble and gentle; be patient, bearing with one another in love." (Ephesians 4:2) I declare that my faith is empathetic and loving.*

Joy

1. *I am a builder of joyful strength. "The joy of the Lord is your strength." (Nehemiah 8:10) I declare that my strength is found in the joy of the Lord.*
2. *I am a builder of joyful praise. "Rejoice in the Lord always. I will say it again: Rejoice!" (Philippians 4:4) I declare that my heart rejoices in the Lord always.*
3. *I am a builder of joy in God's presence. "You make known to me the path of life; you will fill me with joy in your presence, with eternal pleasures at your right hand." (Psalm 16:11)*

I declare that my joy is complete in God's presence.

4. *I am a builder of joy through faith. "May the God of hope fill you with all joy and peace as you trust in him, so that you may overflow with hope by the power of the Holy Spirit." (Romans 15:13)*
   I declare that my faith fills me with joy and peace.
5. *I am a builder of joyful hope. "Be joyful in hope, patient in affliction, faithful in prayer." (Romans 12:12)*
   I declare that my hope is joyful and steadfast.
6. *I am a builder of joy in salvation. "Restore to me the joy of your salvation and grant me a willing spirit, to sustain me." (Psalm 51:12)*
   I declare that my salvation brings me great joy.
7. *I am a builder of joyful thanksgiving. "Give thanks in all circumstances; for this is God's will for you in Christ Jesus." (1 Thessalonians 5:18)*
   I declare that my heart is full of joyful thanksgiving.
8. *I am a builder of joy in God's word. "Your statutes are my heritage forever; they are the joy of my heart." (Psalm 119:111)*
   I declare that God's word is the joy of my heart.
9. *I am a builder of joyful worship. "Worship the Lord with gladness; come before him with joyful songs." (Psalm 100:2)*
   I declare that my worship is filled with joy.
10. *I am a builder of joy in the Holy Spirit. "For the kingdom of God is not a matter of eating and*

drinking, but of righteousness, peace and joy in the Holy Spirit." (Romans 14:17)
I declare that my life is filled with the joy of the Holy Spirit.

11. *I am a builder of joyful strength in the Lord. "The Lord is my strength and my shield; my heart trusts in him, and he helps me. My heart leaps for joy, and with my song I praise him." (Psalm 28:7)*
    I declare that my heart leaps for joy in the Lord.
12. *I am a builder of joyful endurance. "Consider it pure joy, my brothers and sisters, whenever you face trials of many kinds, because you know that the testing of your faith produces perseverance." (James 1:2-3)*
    I declare that my trials produce joy and perseverance.
13. *I am a builder of joyful fellowship. "How good and pleasant it is when God's people live together in unity!" (Psalm 133:1)*
    I declare that my fellowship with others brings joy.
14. *I am a builder of joy in giving. "Each of you should give what you have decided in your heart to give, not reluctantly or under compulsion, for God loves a cheerful giver." (2 Corinthians 9:7)*
    I declare that my giving is done with joy.
15. *I am a builder of joyful obedience. "I take joy in doing your will, my God, for your instructions are written on my heart." (Psalm 40:8)*
    I declare that my obedience brings me joy.

16. *I am a builder of joyful peace. "You will go out in joy and be led forth in peace; the mountains and hills will burst into song before you, and all the trees of the field will clap their hands." (Isaiah 55:12)*
    I declare that my life is led forth in joy and peace.
17. *I am a builder of joy in God's promises. "But be sure to fear the Lord and serve him faithfully with all your heart; consider what great things he has done for you." (1 Samuel 12:24)*
    I declare that my joy is rooted in God's promises.
18. *I am a builder of joyful patience. "Be joyful in hope, patient in affliction, faithful in prayer." (Romans 12:12)*
    I declare that my patience is joyful and enduring.
19. *I am a builder of joy in God's love. "May the Lord direct your hearts into God's love and Christ's perseverance." (2 Thessalonians 3:5)*
    I declare that my joy is found in God's love.
20. *I am a builder of joyful humility. "Humble yourselves before the Lord, and he will lift you up." (James 4:10)*
    I declare that my humility brings joy.
21. *I am a builder of joyful service. "Serve the Lord with gladness; come before his presence with singing." (Psalm 100:2)*
    I declare that my service is done with joy.
22. *I am a builder of joyful contentment. "I have learned to be content whatever the circumstances." (Philippians 4:11)*
    I declare that my contentment brings joy.

23. *I am a builder of joy in God's presence. "You make known to me the path of life; you will fill me with joy in your presence, with eternal pleasures at your right hand." (Psalm 16:11)*
    I declare that my joy is complete in God's presence.
24. *I am a builder of joyful hope. "Be joyful in hope, patient in affliction, faithful in prayer." (Romans 12:12)*
    I declare that my hope is joyful and steadfast.
25. *I am a builder of joyful faith. "The Lord is my strength and my shield; my heart trusts in him, and he helps me. My heart leaps for joy, and with my song I praise him." (Psalm 28:7)*
    I declare that my faith brings me joy.
26. *I am a builder of joyful thanksgiving. "Give thanks in all circumstances; for this is God's will for you in Christ Jesus." (1 Thessalonians 5:18)*
    I declare that my heart is full of joyful thanksgiving.
27. *I am a builder of joyful praise. "Rejoice in the Lord always. I will say it again: Rejoice!" (Philippians 4:4)*
    I declare that my heart rejoices in the Lord always.
28. *I am a builder of joyful trust. "But let all who take refuge in you be glad; let them ever sing for joy. Spread your protection over them, that those who love your name may rejoice in you." (Psalm 5:11)*
    I declare that my trust in God fills me with joy.
29. *I am a builder of joyful encouragement. "Therefore encourage one another and build each other up, just as in fact you are doing."*

(1 Thessalonians 5:11)
I declare that my encouragement brings joy to others.

30. *I am a builder of joyful worship. "Worship the Lord with gladness; come before him with joyful songs." (Psalm 100:2)*
I declare that my worship is filled with joy.
31. *I am a builder of joyful unity. "How good and pleasant it is when God's people live together in unity!" (Psalm 133:1)*
I declare that my unity with others brings joy.

Conclusion: Embracing the Builder Identity

The journey through the pages of this book: **"Be a Builder in the Kingdom: *The C.E.M.E.N.T. Guide to Creating a Lasting Legacy,"*** has illuminated the profound and sacred calling of being a builder in the Kingdom of God. As we conclude, it is essential to internalize the identity of a builder, understanding that this role is not just a task but a divine mandate imbued with eternal significance.

Embracing the Builder Identity

Recognizing oneself as a builder in the Kingdom is a transformative realization. This identity is not limited to constructing physical structures but encompasses every aspect of creating, nurturing, and sustaining God's work on earth. As God's children, made in His image, we inherit His creative and constructive nature. Hebrews 3:3-4 reminds us that God is the ultimate builder, and by His grace, we too are called to build.

Biblical Reflection:

Consider the parable of the talents in Matthew 25:14-30. Each servant was entrusted with resources, and those who invested and built upon their talents were commended. This parable underscores the importance of using what God has given us to build and expand His Kingdom.

Example:

Sarah, a young woman in her local church, felt a strong burden for the children in her community. Recognizing the lack of spiritual education and engagement, she decided to start a Sunday school program. Despite initial challenges and limited resources, Sarah persevered. She sought guidance from God, planned meticulously, and involved other members of the church. Today, the Sunday school is thriving, touching the lives of many children and their families. Sarah's journey exemplifies embracing the builder identity, using her talents to create something enduring and impactful.

Leaving a Lasting Legacy

Building with a Kingdom mindset is about more than just creating something for today; it is about leaving a legacy that honors God and impacts future generations. Our work should reflect the eternal nature of God's Kingdom, aiming to create lasting change and enduring testimony of God's love and power.

Biblical Reflection:

In Genesis 12:2, God's promise to Abraham included making his name great and being a blessing to all nations. Abraham's legacy is not just his physical descendants but also his faith and obedience, which have had a lasting impact on the world.

Example:

Consider the legacy of Billy Graham, who built an extensive ministry based on evangelism. His dedication to spreading the Gospel led to millions hearing the message of Christ, and his legacy continues through the lives changed by his ministry and the ongoing work of the Billy Graham Evangelistic Association.

Action Plan:

- ✓ Reflect on Your Legacy: Spend time in prayer, asking God to reveal the lasting impact He wants you to have. Write down your vision for your legacy and the steps you need to take to achieve it.

- ✓ Engage in Continuous Learning: Stay committed to growing in your faith and understanding of God's Word. Attend Bible studies, read theological books, and seek mentorship from mature Christians.
- ✓ Invest in Others: Part of leaving a legacy is investing in the lives of others. Mentor younger believers, serve in your church, and share your experiences and knowledge.

Call to Action: Inspiring Readers to Start Their Building Journey Today

Now is the time to take up the mantle of building in God's Kingdom. The call to action is not just an invitation but a challenge to step out in faith, trust in God's provision, and begin building with purpose and passion.

Biblical Reflection:

James 2:17 reminds us that faith without works is dead. Our faith in God should propel us into action, driving us to build and create for His glory.

Example:

John, a successful businessman, felt called to use his resources to build a community center in a disadvantaged neighborhood. Despite facing numerous obstacles, John persisted, believing that God had given him this vision. Today, the community center provides educational programs, job training, and a safe space for youth. John's story is a testament to what can be accomplished when we step out in faith and take action.

Action Plan:

- ✓ Identify Your Project: Pray and seek God's guidance to identify the specific project He is calling you to build. It could be a ministry, a community initiative, or a personal endeavor that aligns with His Kingdom purposes.

- ✓ Develop a Detailed Plan: Outline the steps needed to bring your vision to life. Consider the resources required, potential challenges, and timelines. Write everything down and seek advice from trusted mentors.
- ✓ Take the First Step: Start with small, manageable actions. Trust in God's provision and guidance as you begin your building journey. Remember that every great work starts with a single step of faith.
- ✓ Maintain and Grow: Regularly review your progress and make adjustments as needed. Stay committed to prayer and seeking God's wisdom. Celebrate milestones and continue to invest in your project for sustained growth.
- ✓ Share Your Journey: Encourage others by sharing your experiences, challenges, and victories. Your testimony can inspire others to take up their own building projects in God's Kingdom.

By following these practical steps you can confidently embrace your identity as a builder in God's Kingdom. Remember, the journey of building is not just about creating structures but about partnering with God to impact lives, communities, and the world for His glory.

Let your work be a testament to His greatness, leaving a legacy that endures for generations.

About the Author
'GERARD ASSEY'

Gerard Assey is a Graduate in Economics, a PGD in Management (HRD) and holds a Doctorate in Leadership. Gerard holds several International Qualifications in Sales, Debt Collection, Training & Teaching, and is a 'Fellow' of the prestigious 'Institute of Sales & Marketing Management'-UK, a Certified NLP Practitioner, a 'Certified Trainer', an 'Accredited Management Teacher-Behavioral Sciences', a 'Certified Competency Facilitator', a 'Certified Management Consultant'- (the International credentials of a professional management consultant, awarded in accordance with global standards of the ICMCI); and a Certification from the University of Michigan in 'Successful Negotiation: Essential Strategies and Skills'

He is also a Member of the 'National Association of Sales Professionals' backed with several years experience in varied industries, both in India and Overseas. He also holds an 'Etiquette Consultant' Certification from the USA (by Sue Fox, Author of Best Seller: 'Business Etiquette for Dummies'. She has trained some of the top celebrities' world over). He was also a recipient of a scholarship for extensive training in Japan on 'Corporate Management for India'.

Gerard Assey is 'Founder & Chief Corporate Trainer' of the Group: '**Citius, Altius, Fortius Unlimited**'- an organization that **celebrated 20 years of Glorious Service** in 2021, focusing on 3 Core Competencies:

People. Performance. Profit; in functional areas of Sales & Marketing, HR & Organizational Development, covering Recruitment, Training & Consultancy!

Having managed organizations with large Sales Forces in India & Overseas, his specialization cover extensive areas of Sales Training (All levels - Presentation, Negotiation, Key/ Strategic Accounts Management & Managerial Skills for all sectors), Bid Proposal/ Capture Planning/ Management Trainings, Retail Sales, Customer Service & Customer Retention Programs, Training for Prevention & Collection of Debt, Self & Personal Development Programs (Time Management, Teamwork & Team Building, Business Etiquette & Personal Grooming, Leadership & Managerial Skills, People Management Skills, Train-the-Trainer etc), including preparation of Custom-designed Business Manuals for Internal (HR, Induction, and Sales etc) & External use (Instruction, User Manuals).

Gerard has successfully conducted over 6440 Trainings & Workshops (as of Mar '25) all across India, Middle East, Africa, Europe & S.E. Asia. Besides public programs conducted regularly, both in India & Overseas, he has some of the top names as clients whom he services from Single Owners to large Public & Government undertakings, covering all sectors, for their in-house needs.

His website: www.CollectionSkills.com is the only one in this part of the world to be featured in the 'Collections & Credit Risk Magazine-USA' under 'Who's Who in Training' and ranks TOP, along with other websites listed below on most search engines.

Gerard is author of 176 books already (Mar 2025), all the books being available on all online platforms and outlets as E-books and Paperbacks

A few of our business related books:

1. Bite-sized Bits on Commonsense Management
2. Heart to Heart on Life's Principles'
3. How to become a Successful Manager
4. The Sales Professionals' Master Workbook of S.Y.S.T.E.M.S
5. The Professional Business Email Etiquette Handbook & Guide
6. The Professional Business Video-Conferencing Etiquette Handbook & Guide
7. Professional Presentation Skills
8. Exceptional Customer Service
9. Professional Tele-Marketing Skills
10. Professional Debt Collection Skills
11. The G.R.E.A.T. Sales & Service Workbook
12. Sales Training Advantage for Results (*The Ultimate Sales Training Manual to enable you stand out as a S.T.A.R.*)
13. CEO Daily Planner & Organizer
14. The Sales Professionals' Master Daily Planner
15. The Professional Debt Collector's Master Daily Planner
16. My Daily Planner & Organizer
17. MY EMERGENCY INFORMATION RECORD (Family Emergency & Peace of Mind Planner)
18. The Ultimate Therapist & Counselors Planner and Organizer
19. Building an Ethical Workplace
20. Managing Relationships at Work
21. Managing Business Meetings Effectively
22. Effective Delegation Skills
23. Goal Setting for Success
24. B2B Selling by Email
25. Professional Business Etiquette & Grooming
26. Dining Etiquette & Table Manners
27. Effective Networking Skills
28. Grooming, Etiquette & Manners for Teens, Young Adults & Future Leaders
29. Inter-Personal Skills
30. Get Ready, Get Hired!
31. Selling in a Recession

32. Effective Receivables Management in an Economic Downturn!
33. Real Estate & Property Sales Training
34. Credit Sales & Accounts Receivable Management
35. Selling Skills for Real Estate & Property Advisors
36. Take G.R.E.A.T. C.A.R.E!
37. Spa, Salon & Health Club Selling Skills
38. Selling Travel, Holiday & MICE Services
39. Selling Skills for Spa's, Salons & Health Clubs
40. Retailing in Salons & Spas
41. Selling Holiday, Vacation, Tours & Packages
42. The Power of Sales Referrals
43. Selling Luxury
44. Technical Selling Skills
45. Financial Advisors Sales Training
46. Dealing with Burnout at Work Monopolize Your Markets
47. Selling to Affluent Customers
48. Growing up with Grace
49. Financial Selling Skills
50. *The Effective Manager's Guide: Key Skills to Thrive*
51. From Aspiring to Inspiring: A Guide for New Managers on the Rise
52. The Power of Focus
53. Selling with Integrity: Sell Like Jesus The Perfect Role Model!
54. 31 Habits of Champions: Your 31-Day Journey to Greatness
55. Rejecting Grasshopper Talk: From Grasshopper to Giant-Killer-*Defeating Giants Daily!*
56. Navigate the AI-Powered Future of Bid & Proposals: Up-Skill to Stay Relevant with Alternative Career Paths & Opportunities
57. Hiring Sales Winners
58. Present with Impact
59. Success Unlocked: *Breaking Free from Habits that Hold You Back*
60. Complaints to Cheers, Feedback to Gold: Mastering Complaints Management
61. Thriving Together: *Cultivating Diversity, Equity, and Inclusion*
62. Coaching Skills for Sales Managers

63. Soaring to Success in Business & Leadership: Swifter, Higher, Stronger!
64. From Classroom to Podium: A Student's Guide to Powerful Public Speaking & Presentation Skills
65. Developing Self-Discipline
66. The CEO's 31-Day Power Plan: Unlocking Success through Essential Traits
67. Credibility Matters
68. A Winning Attitude
69. Bid & Proposal Management Using AI
70. Sales Forecasting: A Practical & Proven Guide to Strategic Sales Forecasting
71. Elevate & Energize: *50 Dynamic & Fun Activities for Peak Workplace Morale*
72. 'Sales SOS! Sales on Fire! *30 Days to Conquer Chaos & the Nightmares of Success!'*
73. Mastering Sales Managerial Skills: *Building High-Performing Teams & Driving Exceptional Results*
74. Eagle-Eyed Leadership: Unleashing the Power of 31 Lessons from Eagles
75. The Ultimate Employee Training Guide: *Training Today, Leading Tomorrow*
76. Being More Accountable at Work
77. Creating a Culture of Continuous Improvement
78. Effective Questioning & Listening Skills
79. The Power of Value Selling
80. The Growth Mindset
81. Mastering Professional Help Desk Skills
82. The Power to Lead with Empathy
83. Being Prepared: The Key to Unlocking Success
84. Youthful Spark-Youth Energizers, Activities and Games-Igniting the Fun in Youth
85. Ignite your Motivation for Success
86. Elevate Your Executive Presence: *Your Roadmap to Executive Excellence*
87. Smart Decisions: *Mastering Problem Solving with Strategic Solutions for Business Success*
88. Strategic Planning: *Developing and Implementing Strategic Plans to Achieve Long-Term Business Goals*
89. The Power of Stay Interviews
90. Developing G.R.I.T.
91. Adaptability

92. Diagnosis- *A Key Skill for Leadership*
93. The Burnout-Proof Salesperson: *The Master Guide to Preventing Stress & Burnout*- Strategies for Thriving in Sales
94. Learning from Failure: *Keys to Success*
95. Customer Success Management
96. Overcoming the Killers of Motivation
97. The C-Suite Code: *Mastering Skills for Executive Excellence'*
98. Dealing with Difficult Customers
99. Unlocking Your Potential: Mastering the Top 20 Life Skills for a Brighter Future
100. Nurturing Tomorrow's Leaders: *Essential Soft Skills Every Child Must Learn*
101. Lively & Fun Party Games for Seniors & Elders
102. Role Playing for Sales Champions: From Practice to Performance
103. Fun and Exciting Party Games for Kids
104. Case Studies for Sales
105. Role-Playing for Unbeatable Customer Service
106. Case Studies in Customer Service
107. Case Studies in Winning Negotiations
108. Case Studies in Management & Leadership
109. Case Studies in Human Resources & Talent Management
110. CEO Success Blueprint: The Essential Toolkit for CEOs and C-Level Executives
111. The Salesperson's Self-Coaching Guide: *Master Your Own Self-Coaching Plan for Success*
112. Overcoming Procrastination: *Your Ultimate Guide to Stop Delaying and Start Living Your Best Life*
113. When True Colors Are Exposed: *The Journey to Unmasking Humanity*
114. Life-Changing Habits for Teens: Teen Success Blueprint for a Bright Future
115. Workplace Stress-Free: *Proven Strategies to Thrive at Work and Beyond*

From the Ministry side, Gerard graduated in the very first batch of Charis Bible College-India & had for over 9 years served as a Part-time Faculty at Charis Bible College-Chennai (Andrew Wommack Ministries-Colorado, USA).
He is also a graduate of the Advanced Mentorship Program (AMP) and the Circle Of Ministerial Engagement (C.O.M.E.) of Prophet Jerome Fernando and a Spiritual Son of the Esteemed Prophet.
An accomplished author of several Secular & Christian Books, Gerard has been on the board of a few international organizations and boasts of being the SON of the MOST HIGH GOD: An ordinary guy following an extraordinary GOD!

...And some of his most recent Christian Books being:

1. A Bouquet of Praises for My KING
2. Christian Jokes for the Serious Religious' Folks!
3. Jesus Healed You!
4. Praise24Ever! (also in Tamil version)
5. The 5G Network of GOD
6. Building Faith over F.E.A.R- FACE EVERYTHING AND RISE with JESUS
7. Hebrew and Greek Praise and Worship Words
8. Godly Mothers' and Grandmothers' Bible Story time for Kids!
9. Miracles of Jesus in Pictures
10. Raise your Praise all 365 Days
11. Thanking GOD with an Attitude of Gratitude
12. Meditating on the Attributes of GOD
13. Puppet Scripts
14. Alcohol Ruins, JESUS Reforms, Renews & Restores!
15. Habakkuk 2:2 Christian Daily Journal, Planner & Organizer
16. ABC of GOD's Word for Handwriting Practice
17. Daily Bible Verse Handwriting Practice (Building Godly Character & Faith through Cursive Handwriting Practice!)
18. Guiding Light: Fun & Faith-Building Bible Activities for Children
19. Rejecting Grasshopper Talk: From Grasshopper to Giant-Killer-*Defeating Giants Daily!*
20. Teen Titans of Faith: *Building Courage, Determination & Christ-like-Esteem*
21. I AM Empowered: *Unleashing Divine Power with Positive Declarations*
22. Be A Solution Provider-*From Passion to Purpose*: *A Biblical Guide to Being the Answer to the World!*
23. Miracles of JESUS

24. Parables of Jesus for a Meaningful Life!
25. A Grateful Heart: Importance of Sharing Testimonies of GOD's Grace
26. Melodies of Worship to JESUS: 31 Songs of Praise & Worship From My Heart to HIS!
27. I AM SO BLESSED!
28. My Daily Cup of Energizer
29. 31 Leadership Lessons *from* Jesus- *The Supreme Leader*
30. Peace Amidst Storms: A Biblical Guide to Conquering S.T.R.E.S.S.
31. Rise Above: 20 Biblical Eagle Lessons for Life's Triumphs
32. Godly Goal Setting: *The FAITHFUL Blueprint for a Purpose-Driven Life*
33. The Profound Attributes of our Mighty GOD: Understanding the 10S's of the Almighty
34. Worship Now, Worship Forever: *A Journey from Earthly Praise to Eternal Glory*
35. Unceasing Praise & Worship: *365 Days to Worship the King*
36. The ROAR Within: *Living with Purpose and Authority through the Power of the Holy Spirit*
37. From Potential to Purpose: Unlocking and Multiplying Your Talents & Gifts for Kingdom Impact
38. Songs from the Heart: *Worshipping GOD in Your Own Tune & Melody*
39. Awakening Praise & Worship: Hebrew & Greek Words to Raise Your Praise
40. Sing a NEW Song to the LORD Everyday: *Daily Devotions of Praise & Worship to Lift Your Heart & Glorify HIS Name*
41. *The* A.R.O.M.A. of True Worship: *Creating Worship That Delights God*
42. Becoming A Kingdom Champion: *Embracing God's Call for a Life of Purpose & Victory*
43. The Busy Businessman's Daily Devotional: 366 Crisp Truths to Start Your Day Strong
44. The Teacher's Heart: *Daily Devotions for Educators*
45. Anchored! *A 31-Day Devotional for Students Facing Life's Challenges*
46. Suddenly! Unlocking Unorthodox Breakthroughs through Unusual Worship
47. Overcoming Adversity: *Lessons from the Bible for Modern Challenges*
48. LORD, Don't do it without me
49. Kingdom Leadership: *Biblical Principles for Modern Leaders*
50. Heartprints of God- *Growing God's Way:* Daily Devotions for Kids

to Shine Bright

51. Send Judah First: Let your Praises Go up First to See the Mighty Move of GOD
52. DIVINE MOMENTS: *Recognizing, Embracing, Preparing, and Walking into Life-Changing Encounters with God*
53. Be a Builder in the Kingdom: *The C.E.M.E.N.T. Guide to Creating a Lasting Legacy*

Besides regularly contributing to business & trade journals, including international ones such as the 'Creative Training Techniques' and the 'Sales News' of the U.S.A, He is also a member of several prestigious bodies & trade associations, having participated in many Conferences & Workshops in India & Overseas.

Prior to his last assignment of leading & managing a large MNC as head, Gerard had a 3-year stint in the Middle East as a Consultant with a leading British Consultancy Firm.

As the past 'Official Country Representative' for the International Business Award- 'THE STEVIES'-(the business world's own Oscar) for about 4 years- he ensured a few Indian companies that qualify for the same every year!

Gerard can be contacted at:
Email: training@Sales-Training.in,training@CollectionSkills.com
Websites:

www.Sales-Training.in
www.EtiquetteWorks.in
www.CollectionSkills.com
www.RetailSalesTraining.in
www.SalesTrainingIndia.com
www.ManualPreparation.com
www.TrainingWithPuppets.com
www.FirstContactAcademy.com
www.SalesAndMarketingRecruiter.com

Our TRAININGS that can help your team

- ✓ **Sales Effectiveness**: Selling Skills for any Sector: Service/ Logistics/ FMCG Realty/ Insurance & Finance/ Media/ SPA's, Health Clubs & Salons/ Key Account Management, Effective Negotiation Skills/ Bid & Proposal Management Skills/ Retail Sales Training: Any Sector (Auto, Jewelry, Clothing, Luxury etc)
- ✓ **Customer Service Skills**-Complaints Handling & Customer Retention
- ✓ **Debt Prevention & Collection Skills**
- ✓ **Etiquette & Grooming**
- ✓ **Leadership & Managerial Skills**
- ✓ **Self & Personal Development Skills**: Presentation Skills/ Effective Communication Skills/Business Proposal Writing Skills/ Problem Solving & Decision Making Skills/ Empowering Secretaries-The perfect PA! (For Secretaries & PA's)/ Effective Time Management/ Teamwork & Teambuilding/ P.R.I.D.E- **P**ersonal **R**esponsibility **I**n **D**elivering **E**xcellence

www.ingramcontent.com/pod-product-compliance
Ingram Content Group UK Ltd.
Pitfield, Milton Keynes, MK11 3LW, UK
UKHW021339190726
13845UKWH00027B/636

9 788197 436932